The Best of BERTHA MUNRO

First Time in Print

In 1899 a letter from a 12-year-old girl was printed in the *Beulah Christian*. It read: "Dear *Beulah Christian,* Our minister was telling us that you would like to have some of the children write to the *Beulah Christian* and tell what Jesus has done for them. So I am going to because Jesus has done so much for me. He saved me when I was 10 years old, and after that He gave me a clean heart. He has come to abide in my heart, and I do love Him better than anyone else in the world. Yours in Jesus. Bertha Munro."

From the *Christian Scholar,* Memorial Edition, February 1983, published by Eastern Nazarene College, Quincy, Mass.

The Best of
Bertha Munro

Edited, with Introduction by

Earl C. Wolf

Memorial Edition

Beacon Hill Press of Kansas City
Kansas City, Missouri

ISBN: 083-411-1403

Printed in the
United States of America

Cover: Royce Ratcliff

Permission to quote from the following copyrighted versions are acknowledged with appreciation:

The Holy Bible, New International Version (NIV), copyright © 1973, 1978, 1984 by the International Bible Society.

The New Testament in Modern English (Phillips), Revised Edition © J. B. Phillips, 1958, 1960, 1972. By permission of the Macmillan Publishing Co.

10 9 8 7 6 5 4 3 2 1

Contents

Foreword

James Garfield, in an address to the alumni of Williams College, said,

> I am not willing that this discussion should close without mention of the value of a true teacher. Give me a log hut, with only a simple bench, Mark Hopkins on one end and I on the other, and you may have all the buildings, apparatus, and libraries without him.

Bertha Munro was that kind of teacher. During her many years of teaching at Eastern Nazarene College, students flocked to her classes. The "lit major" became the most popular course of study because she made literature live for her students. And, as you will see in the pages of this book, she applied a scholarly knowledge of her discipline to the living of the Christian life, offering examples from great literature that vividly illustrated biblical truth.

Although, rightly, most of those who knew Dean Munro felt that they had a very special relationship with her, it was my privilege to know her intimately as "Auntie Bertie," and to be the recipient of her love and wisdom as if I were her son. As I have read and reread her words, selected with loving care by her former student, Dr. Earl C. Wolf, she seems to live again. I marvel anew at her ability to bring God's truth to bear upon the human condition in our day.

As we now observe the 100th anniversary of her birth, it is my heartfelt prayer that *The Best of Bertha Munro* may again minister to men and women, challenging all who read to follow her example and give their best in service to Jesus Christ, His Church, and His kingdom.

—STEPHEN W. NEASE

Introduction

This book is not an attempt to present a biography of Dean Bertha Munro. With the exception of her retirement years, she has done that herself in her autobiography, *The Years Teach.* This book is an effort to capture the melody of a life after the singer has gone, to grasp anew the spirit of one who now lives triumphantly in God's eternal day.

Miss Munro was a staunch Christian, professor of English literature and academic dean at Eastern Nazarene College for most of her 65 years of teaching, and lay theologian and Christian scholar. This book seeks to present reflections of her life through her writings.

For more than 13 years Dean Munro wrote a column for her denominational teachers' magazine, first under the heading "Points That Are Practical" and then as "Truth for Today." For several years she contributed monthly articles for the youth magazine *Conquest* and a regular column titled "Thought for the Day" in the *Herald of Holiness.* She contributed also to ENC's college paper, *Christian Scholar,* and to other magazines and publications of her denomination. Without doubt the best of these works were put into her books, the first of which, *Truth for Today,* was published in 1947 by her denominational publishing house—as were all her books.

From that first book we follow chronologically her publications for the choice selections of her writings. There are, however, the three last sections—Other Writings, A Collection of Gems, and The Bible as Literature—that do not follow strictly the chronological pattern.

Most likely we have not included everything that all readers would consider best. But we trust that our considered selections are *among the best* of Dean Munro's writings.

Truth for Today (1947). The devotionals in this book are based on the writings in the teachers' magazine and dedicated "to my coworkers, the Sunday School teachers of the Church of the Nazarene, who gave me the original inspiration for these notes." This devotional book—and its companion volume, *Strength for Today*—extended Dean Munro's ministry beyond thousands of students to thousands of homes where families have been inspired to seek earnestly to know and do the will of God.

Not Somehow, but Triumphantly (1950). Appearing first in *Conquest,* here are some of Miss Munro's choice chapel talks to young people. She dedicated this book "to the young people who inspired it." Of the title she says, "I did not even choose the phrase; it chose me, forced itself on me when I saw it on a little shield motto in the office of President Young's secretary. From that moment on I could never escape it" *(The Years Teach).*

The Pilgrim's Road Map (1950). This book was based on John Bunyan's Christian classic, *Pilgrim's Progress,* and was dedicated "to the memory of *My Mother,* who made my childhood Sunday afternoons happy by reading *Pilgrim's Progress.*"

Strength for Today (1954). This companion volume to *Truth for Today* was dedicated "to my Sunday School girls of the years, now scattered abroad, who have taught me much."

The Years Teach (1974). This autobiography, written at the request of her former students, is dedicated "to ENC Alumni, old and new, far and near, for whom this book is written."

Shining Pathway: Mini-Devotionals for People on the Go (1974). Written after her retirement from teaching in 1968, Dean Munro says of the title, "I did not choose the title of this book; it chose me. Of recent years I have found myself depending personally without question on God's statement of fact in Prov. 4:18: 'The path of the just [obedient] is as the shining light, that shineth more and more unto the perfect day.' . . . I have never forgotten the shining pathway—I trust I never shall."

Dean Munro was counselor to thousands of students during her years of teaching at ENC (1919-68). After her retirement she continued to keep in touch with countless students through correspondence. Even after her homegoing on January 19, 1983, her letter-writing ministry found an extension through the publication of *One in the Bond of Love,* by Hazel C. Lee. Preserved in this book are letters from Bertha Munro to her former student, Dr. Earl G. Lee, pastor for 18 years of the First Church of the Nazarene, Pasadena, Calif., in response to sermons shared through his tape ministry.

Mrs. Hazel Lee, also a former student and admirer, took the 67 letters written from Miss Munro to her husband and selected the best of these communications from what she calls the "slowing ebb time" of Miss Munro's life.

Sprinkled throughout Dean Munro's publications are a number of terse statements—so characteristic of her writing. She was gifted in putting into brief form great truths— distillations of wisdom. A few of these are put together under the caption "A Collection of Gems."

I am indebted to Dr. Stephen W. Nease, president of Eastern Nazarene College, for providing the Foreword and the content of chapters 11 and 12 of this memorial volume.

—EARL C. WOLF

The Best of BERTHA MUNRO

1

Devotional Writings

Christ—What Then?

Matt. 2:9-11; John 7:32-39; 10:19-30

He that believeth on me, as the scripture hath said, out of his [innermost being] shall flow rivers of living water (John 7:38).

The world is full of notions about religion. The birth of Jesus shows us what real religion is. Religion is not a human scheme. It is not "God made in the image of man." It is revelation from above; there was light from a star. It is power from above; there was a Heavenly Child born. God made the first move.

Real religion is not cold creed. It has a creed, but it starts with personal experience. For it begins with the love that sent Jesus to earth, and the heart hunger that sent the Magi journeying. It is consummated when that hunger meets that love.

Real religion is more than formal ritual in a fine church. The Christian religion began in a stable where the only form was spontaneous adoration. It began when men met God sincerely. It continues so.

Real religion has at least three elements: heart satisfaction (a personal seeking and finding of God); worship (a personal adoring of God); consecration (a personal giving to God). Real religion is a personal relationship. Wise men will recognize Christ; they will worship; they will give. A test for every one of us.

What have I to give my Lord? Just what the wise men gave. Gold—all the things that are wealth to me: money and health and strength and friends. Frankincense—the first intensity of my heart's love and loyalty. Myrrh—my sorrows, my hurts, my trials—and my power to suffer. When I give Him these, I give Him all. And He is worthy.

> *Well of water, ever springing,*
> *Bread of life, so rich and free,*
> *Untold wealth that never faileth,*
> *My Redeemer is to me.*

The New Commandment

John 15:10-12; Gal. 5:13-15

These things have I spoken unto you, that my joy might remain in you, and that your joy might be full (John 15:11).

The new commandment is the best way. Love is the normal way. Supernaturally natural, it is furnished from above. One glimpse of the Cross, and love springs up for the God who "so loved the world," for the Christ who "gave himself for me," for the others for whom He died. Grateful love and deeds that show it are spontaneous, natural. Gratitude is no burden for the man who has been redeemed; formal obedience would mark him a base ingrate.

Love is the formal *family atmosphere,* and the family is the normal unit of human society. As Christians we belong to a heavenly family unit. That family will never be torn apart by war, never invaded by death. Let us cultivate those family ties that cannot be broken.

Love is the *joyful* way of living. Try it and see. Jesus was the Great Lover; and He had joy to give away.

Our joy in loving is not gay cheer, not even the natural pleasure of making others happy. It is Jesus' joy that He gives us, a deep calm, independent of circumstances or people's appreciation. If we love God and our neighbor in His way,

18

His joy remains whether God treats us as it seems He should, or not; whether people praise us or blame us.

Jesus' joy is not natural to us, but it fits our natures. His joy makes our joy full. It is what we have been looking for all our lives. Would you know satisfaction? Then learn to live by love.

> *Living for Jesus, oh, what rest!*
> *Pleasing my Saviour, I am blest.*

Great Moments

Mark 9:2-8

They saw no man any more, save Jesus only with themselves (Mark 9:8).

Life's great moments are its high mountains. In every Christian experience there are a few great moments that stand out from all the rest, moments that have changed the course of our lives. They are the moments when we have managed to forget our crowd and their ideas, ourselves and our own wishes, and got a revelation of God and His truth and His will for us, of Jesus Christ and His love and its meaning for us. We saw the Cross; we saw heaven. We breathed heavenly air and looked from a higher point of view. That view has not changed; only we have come down into the dust and confusion.

They are poor indeed who never have had great moments of revelation. Great moments are reality. For behind the scenes is eternity. Faith is not believing what isn't so. It is shutting your ears to all the lying things that are not so, and opening your eyes to the things that are gloriously, eternally real. Faith sees Jesus.

Faith is living logically. *If* the unseen, eternal things are the real and lasting, what then? *If* Jesus is God and is with me always, then how should I live? Faith dares be consistent. Faith accepts the challenge and lives as if Jesus were who He is.

> *Since my eyes were fixed on Jesus,*
> *I've lost sight of all beside;*
> *So enchained my spirit's vision,*
> *Looking at the Crucified.*

A Second-Generation Christian

Gen. 26:26-30

We saw certainly that the Lord was with thee (Gen. 26:28).

The story of Isaac is the story of a conqueror who won out by holding on. The inner victory comes always before the outer. If the circumstances of life are proving too much for you, get a fresh vision of God, a fresh sense of His presence, a fresh reminder of His unchanged covenant. It is like God to give you that assurance after trial and patient endurance. Then,

> *Keep holding on, keep holding on,*
> *The victory will soon be won.*

Hold on with confidence. It is astonishing how quickly things work out once you get the victory in your own soul over your circumstances.

Hold on when your persecutors are the most provoking. If you can stand it a moment longer, you will find they were

20

just on the point of yielding when you thought them the strongest.

Hold on until your enemies can see how your God has delivered you. Sinners admire a Christian when they have tried him out, and they are convicted of their own need. This trial is your opportunity to glorify God. Perhaps you will never have another like it. Hold on a little longer.

> *He'll take you through, however you're tried,*
> *His tender care is never denied;*
> *Then always trust His promise so true—*
> *He'll take you through.*

The Last Week

Matt. 22:1-10; 26:6-16, 69-75

Wheresoever this gospel shall be preached in the whole world, there shall also this, that this woman hath done, be told for a memorial of her (Matt. 26:13).

We realize the omnipotence of free choice. There are the *excusers:* the indifferent many whose lives are too full to have room for Christ and His blessing. They hear the gospel call, but they ask to be excused. Excused from what? From eternal life and everlasting joy.

There is the *traitor,* who deliberately sold his Lord. Impossible! Yet a habit of compromise, a self-deception that tries to serve God and Mammon, will blind the eyes and callous the heart until men do things they never would have dreamed of. Lucifer was once an angel.

There are the *loyal few.* They do not understand; they are bewildered by the storm. But they know they love their Lord and trust His love. They fail and falter, sometimes when He needs them most. But they have learned one thing: They cannot live without Him. If they stand by long enough and claim His promise, they will receive the stabilizing gift of the Holy Spirit.

Out of the groups stand *individuals.* Jesus knows me by my name. I can be Mary, forgiven much and loving much; or I can be Judas, unappreciative of all He has done for me and all the opportunities He has given me. I can be openhearted Peter, weeping bitterly and repenting sincerely of my sin; or I can be weak Pilate, choosing deliberately to please the crowd rather than Christ, and risking the consequences. No one gives me my name; I choose it myself. But the name I choose here is the name I must be remembered by.

> *My Jesus, I love Thee; I know Thou art mine.*
> *For Thee all the follies of sin I resign.*

The Seven Words
of the Garden

Matt. 26:39, 42

Nevertheless not my will, but thine, be done (Luke 22:42).

"If it be possible ... nevertheless ... thy will be done" —*Jesus' Submission.* In Jesus' prayer the struggle and the yielding came in the same breath; the personal request and the choice of the Father's will. It should always be so. Never risk asking God for anything without quickly adding, "If it be Thy will."

The will of God was Jesus' passion; He came to earth to do it. And the will of God is the ruling principle of every sanctified man's life.

This word of submission does not mean that heart and flesh may not be torn with unspeakable anguish at the cost of our "yes." Jesus was human as well as divine, and we are human. The devil will taunt us for our weakness; Jesus will understand.

The steps of praying through a personal problem: (1) Love the will of God. (2) Make sure of the will of God. (3) Rest in the will of God. (4) Do the will of God. And remember, "The love of God is always wise."

How glad I am that Jesus did not choose selfishly in Gethsemane; there would have been no hope for my soul. And today perhaps some soul is depending on me not to choose selfishly. I can be sure of it, for God does not waste sacrifice. He will use what I give.

> *My Jesus, as Thou wilt;*
> *O may Thy will be mine!*
> *Into Thy hand of love*
> *I would my all resign.*

The Risen Lord

John 20:1-3; Isa. 53:9-12

And they found the stone rolled away from the sepulchre (Luke 24:2).

God does not stop working when things look hopeless.

The Stone Rolled Away. Our enemies are not so powerful, after all. Not when God takes hold of us. Our case seems hopeless—but God is not dead.

Someone has tampered with death—that Someone is God! Death is not final. No longer need we feel when we lay our loved ones in the grave that the last word has been spoken. There is One whose finger will roll away the stone, as a very little thing.

The Empty Tomb. God's Son has died under a cloud; He will not leave His name smirched as an impostor and a deceiver. All the world can know, if they will. Satan still is clouding His name and casting doubts on His faithfulness. But God is the same. One day the justification will be full and complete. All shall see Him exalted. We shall be there.

The Jesus who called back Lazarus, the Christ who promised eternal life—what is He doing in the tomb? Get your share of His eternal life, and you too will be out of place in the grave.

> *Let me, like Mary, through the gloom*
> *Come with a gift to Thee.*
> *Show to me now the empty tomb;*
> *Lead me to Calvary.*

Jesus with Us

John 20:19-20; 21:4-13

Came Jesus and stood in the midst (John 20:19).

"Jesus in the midst" of our gatherings, social as well as definitely sacred—would our words, our acts, our feelings even, have a different color or a gentler tone? He is there so long as we are truly Christian. Let us recognize His presence and do Him the kind of honor He seeks.

One of our greatest essayists writes that if Shakespeare should come into the room where a group of literary men are assembled, they would all rise to honor him. But if Jesus Christ were to enter, they would all kneel and kiss the hem of His garment. Do you feel that way? Is He greater than all the great to you? Cultivate the passionate homage of your soul to Jesus. He is worthy.

Jesus is not dead. He is not a name only, not a historic fact only, not a beautiful life only, not a removed distant atonement only. He is living: He is Person; High Priest, and, through the Spirit, Companion, Friend, Counselor, Great Lover. I can talk with Him—I do. He can talk with me—He does. That living fellowship has implications that I must realize—or He is as good as dead to me.

> *Then I saw at once that Jesus*
> *Could be better far than all:*
> *He could lighten up the pathway,*
> *Could surround me like a wall;*
> *He could take the place of loved ones*
> *Wipe the falling tears away,*
> *Turn my sorrow into laughter,*
> *Change my nighttime into day.*

I Should Be My Best

Gen. 2:4-17

God created man in his own image (Gen. 1:27).

Because of what I am: my possibilities. Made in God's image, I was made to commune with Him. I should not let my program get so full that time for prayer is crowded out. Then my likeness to God is only potential; my soul is stunted.

Made in God's image, I have the faculty of reason, of planning, of purposing. I should allow myself no indulgences that cloud my reason and make me reckless of my choices and my future. Alcohol is one such indulgence; but there are

25

others: pleasure, ambition, moneymaking, human love. I would not "just grow"; I would grow in His image.

Made in God's image, I have the privilege of developing that image in me. God is love; He expresses himself by blessing. I would be that sort of person; I would bring blessing to those I touch. It doesn't come by vaguely wishing.

Because of what I am: my responsibilities. God made man responsible for the earth on which he was placed. Each of us has a plot to till. Each of us has a contribution to make to his generation before he passes on. I have only one life. When I come to the end there will be nothing that I can do about it if the impact of my life has been below par. Today is the time to do my best.

> *Thou of life the Fountain art;*
> *Freely let me take of Thee.*
> *Spring Thou up within my heart;*
> *Rise to all eternity.*

Even as Your Father

Matt. 5:43-48

Be ye therefore perfect, even as your Father which is in heaven is perfect (Matt. 5:48).

God expects us to be godlike. Homer, in his epic poems, when he speaks of a great hero, designates him regularly as "godlike." He has that something in his nature that cannot be explained in terms of ordinary human nature; it raises him above the normal; he is superhuman. So of God's men. We can't excuse ourselves by saying, "It's only human to do thus and so." We are expected to live a life that is stamped with God.

26

The dealings of God with man are based in *moral respon-sibility.* He is holy. God has limited himself to moral right-ness. There are evil things He cannot do because He is him-self. That sense of personal accountability to do the highest good we know is the core of personality, the image of God in the soul. I do not want to deface it. I want no wider liberty. The soul is damned that loses it or casts it off.

God has limited himself by *specific responsibilities:* to ev-ery part of the universe He has made, to every creature of His hand. He is love. So we are bound by responsibilities in every one of life's relationships. For every new situation in life there is a new set of relationships, and so a new set of responsibil-ities. This is what "adjustment" means for Christians. Shifted suddenly from one environment to another? Find your re-sponsibilities: as a man to man, as a Christian to needy souls.

Stamp Thine own image deep on my heart.

Christian Essentials

1 Pet. 4:7-19

Be . . . sober, and watch unto prayer (1 Pet. 4:7).

To the very end of time *the Christian Church is committed to some positive Christian principles.* The Church has the long view and so lives by a different scale of values from the world. Its *summum bonum* is not anything that can be realized in time: not money, not social prestige, but eternal life.

The Christian's *wealth?* Good works here and eternal values laid up in heaven. Are those the investments I am concentrating on?

The Christian's *conduct?* Soberness, prayerfulness, char-ity (love)—the Bible has not a word to say about brilliance or

27

cleverness or "leadership qualities" or "tact" or "social adapt-ability." Am I majoring in the right things?

The Christian's *life?* A fight. The world will never be a friend to grace. I am deceived if I think all is going smoothly; that is my moment of greatest danger. Am I looking for an "easy way"?

The Christian's *attitude to money?* Stewardship. Do I dole out my tithe to the Lord, then lavish the rest on "keeping up with the Joneses"—or leading them? Or do I spend every dime as for the Lord?

The Christian's *ambition?* To make heaven and take as many with him as he can. Am I more interested in anything than I am in saving souls and helping them on their way to heaven?

The Christian's *secret of success?* Faith. Not popular favor, not pull with the great, not his own efforts or his own win-someness, not favorable circumstances. Just his confidence in the God of battles who cannot be defeated. Do I live as if I believed God?

> *If every member were just like me,*
> *What kind of church would my church be?*

The Lord's Day

Matt. 12:1-13

For the Son of man is Lord even of the sabbath day (Matt. 12:8).

We should use Sunday to let our Lord bless us. The Lord's day is a day of privilege as well as debt. How many good gifts of our Lord we shall miss completely if we rob Him of His day.

28

Sunday is the Lord's day; in it Jesus will show His authority over our *minds*. Sunday is a good day to increase my store of truth. Let me go to His house expecting to receive a new revelation of truth direct from Him through His minister. He has it for me; He knows that no secondhand theorizing will serve my need.

Sunday is the Lord's day; in it Jesus shows His authority over our *spirits*. Sunday is a good day to seek deliverance from sin. If the demons of selfishness or pride or envy or worldly ambition have got a grip on my soul anywhere, let me use His day to seek the holiness He offers. He concentrates on setting captive souls at liberty; He is looking my way.

Sunday is the Lord's day; in it Jesus would show His authority over our *bodies*. The best way to keep in good health is to rest one day a week. In the sanctuary, in quiet meditation, you will find poise and refreshment. And if you will give God time to talk to you, you may find Him willing to do some temporal things for you—healing, supply of financial needs, practical guidance—you never could have found in the week's rush.

> *Day of all the week the best,*
> *Emblem of eternal rest.*

The Faith That Saves

Rom. 3:21-31

Christ Jesus: whom God hath set forth to be a propitiation through faith in his blood (Rom. 3:24-25).

My faith has a solid basis—Calvary. "I can trust the Man who died for me." Faith is efficient because it takes my eyes

29

off my weak self and fixes them on my mighty Savior. I have been bitten by the serpent and there is no help in me. I must look to the brazen serpent, symbol of the Great Deliverer.

The cross of Jesus is something more than the place where a good man laid down his life. It is the place where the Son of God bore the sins of the whole world. Mine were included, if I will claim my deliverance. He identified himself there with my sin if I will identify myself with Him now.

Faith is not antinomian; faith in God is not an evasion of God's holy law. Because through faith my sins have been nailed to the cross of Christ I do not look lightly on sin; rather, I loathe it more, for it killed my Lord. Faith links me up with power to keep on the rails of the law.

"The best 'moral man' is a Christless man; the weakest Christian is a man plus Christ—the difference is infinite." —C. W. Butler.

Calvary is enough. If God gave Christ, He will not fail me. Through Calvary, life is related rightly with eternity. To Calvary I pin my faith forever.

> My faith still clings to Calvary,
> Where lifted high upon the tree,
> The Son of God I see.

The Faith That Saves

Eph. 2:8-22

By grace are ye saved through faith (Eph. 2:8).

My faith does something in heaven; it changes my record on the books of heaven. "Who is he that condemneth?" The only One who has a right to speak against me now is the "Christ that died," and He has become my Friend. If Satan reminds me of my past sins, I can remind him that the black past is washed away in the blood of Jesus. It can never be found. The page is clean.

My faith brings me into a new relation with God; I am at peace with Him. "I looked to Him, He looked to me, and we are one forever"—Charles Spurgeon's testimony, and the testimony of every truly believing soul. That is conversion.

My faith does something in me; for gloom and fear and despondency it brings me peace and joy and hope. The Christian hope is a rejoicing thing. Only the believing heart dares look clear through to the end of time.

Faith is positive, certain, sure. The moment faith wavers, doubt has entered and faith is no longer faith.

And "the wireless current that God has chosen for the conveying of His power to the world is our faith"—I. Lilias Trotter.

> *Gone is the night with its shadows drear;*
> *Morning hath dawned upon me.*
> *Gone is the burden of anxious fear;*
> *Freedom my portion shall be.*

Prayer and Thanksgiving

Phil. 4:6-7; 1 Thess. 5:16-18

Pray without ceasing. In every thing give thanks (1 Thess. 5:17-18).

If it seems you have no right to be thankful in an evil world, study Paul's recipes for prayer. There is always a "Thanks be to God" included.

There are four steps in every successful prayer: (1) Stop worrying! (2) Share your problem with God. (3) Give thanks

31

before you feel it. (4) Enjoy the peace that has no human basis—it passes understanding.

There are three life attitudes that combine to make a successful prayer life: (1) the praise habit: keep a song in your heart whatever your circumstances; (2) the prayer habit: count nothing too small to take to God in prayer; (3) the submission habit: take everything that comes to you as from the Lord. With these three habits you are invincible.

True prayer has no whine in it. We can spend hours on our knees rehearsing our worries and feel worse when we get up. We have not prayed a word.

Bishop Quayle tells us how he had been pacing the floor in anxiety for hours when suddenly he stopped short, laughed aloud, and went upstairs to sleep. He had heard God's voice saying, "It's all right now, bishop. You go to bed, and I'll stay up the rest of the night."

What does it mean to me to know that All-power, All-love, All-wisdom is at the other end of my prayer?

I'll drop my burden at His feet,
And bear a song away.

Meeting Life's Problems

Acts 26:9-23; Phil. 3:3-7

Man shall not live by bread alone, but by every word that proceedeth out of the mouth of God (Matt. 4:4).

It is safe to trust God's judgment—always. It is safe to trust *God's knowledge* where we cannot understand. The Bible is a Book of Miracles because every human problem, moral and spiritual, is found there, with its solution. No, your name and address are not there, but your case is there. I challenge you to look for it. The Book was written for you.

It is safe to adopt *God's standards of value* as our own. Jesus settled it to take God's definitions and live by them—so may we. To make lives is more important than to make money.

I am serving a greater than Mammon. I am working for more than money or even position. So I cannot be offended or slighted or starved. God pays my wages.

It is safe to carry out *God's commission* at any price. Jesus settled—so may we—to do God's will whatever the cost. The time comes for all of us to carry out the consecration we made at the altar. Well for us then if we actually died to our own will.

Jesus' commission was a fulfilling of prophecy. So is ours, though not announced so publicly. Every one of us is an essential link in God's plan of saving the world. We have a place to fill. He is counting on us.

We need not feel sorry for ourselves if we accept God's commission for our lives. It will not make us popular with certain groups, but it will make us bringers of blessings to shadowed, captive hearts. It is good news we have to tell.

> *Jesus, I my cross have taken,*
> *All to leave and follow Thee.*

The Christian in the World

1 Pet. 2:9-12; 1:13-17

Ye are a chosen generation, a royal priesthood, an holy nation, a peculiar people (1 Pet. 2:9).

The status of the Christian: a citizen of two worlds. Christians are *holy* people. Their hearts are clean. They have accepted the facts that they must do without anger, jealousy, self-seeking, deceit; that they must work by love, self-denial, kindness, patience. All their distinction is to be in their likeness to Christ. Crucifixion? But the beginning of eternal life.

Christians are *pilgrims*. They are not trying to see how much like the world they can be. They are regulating life and practice by the standards of heaven. They are passing through the world, but they expect to live in heaven, and they want to be at home there. Test your soul habits. Are they good fashion for heaven?

Christians are *fighters*. Not against worldly people, but against the worldly spirit. The world will never help you toward God: the current is all the other way; you will have to swim upstream. Note the definition of worldliness: any desire that "war[s] against the soul"; any practice that hurts your spiritual life. You can tell it.

Christians are *good citizens*. For God is the Author of law and order, and He sponsors it. Laws unjust, rulers arbitrary, but until conscience is violated we owe loyalty and cooperation to those in authority. And He makes it blessedly possible for us to obey even the unreasonable without a servile spirit or a loss of self-respect; for He says that in obeying them we are serving Him. There is always a look beyond.

Though exiled from home, yet still I may sing:
"All glory to God, I'm a child of the King!"

Jesus Says You Should Forgive

Matt. 18:21-35

Forgive us our debts, as we forgive our debtors (Matt. 6:12).

Because God has forgiven you. "Seventy times seven." There can never be an end to your forgiving because there can never be an end to your need of God's forgiveness. Be ungracious to someone—and the next minute you will find yourself having to say, "Pardon me," to someone else, and feeling small. Watch the way it goes. Much more, refuse to forgive someone; very soon you will find yourself needing God's forgiveness—and unable to get it.

"Even as I had pity on thee." How great His mercy to us. We cannot compute our debt. If we lived more in the mood of thankfulness, we should be so conscious of our canceled 10,000-talent debt that we should delight in forgetting the 100 pence our neighbor owes us. When our salvation becomes commonplace to us, our hearts will become hard.

"From your hearts." Every hurt that comes is an opportunity to be like Christ. But the opportunity comes disguised; all we see, for the pain, is the injustice of it. Don't use part of the Atonement only. Let Jesus carry your hurts as well as your sins.

Amazing grace! how sweet the sound!
That saved a wretch like me!

Fishers of Men

Acts 2:37-41; 5:12-16

Fear not; from henceforth thou shalt catch men (Luke 5:10).

Christ promises results. It may take time, but the catch is sure. If He has asked you to preach or to go as a missionary, or just to be a true Christian, you are not called to be a failure or to mark time. His word is not, "Do your best"; not, "Try to catch"; not, "Hold the fishing rod"; but *"Thou shalt catch."*

He makes us fishers of men by His blessing. But we have to do the fishing. We have to cast the spiritual net and bait the spiritual hooks and use all the fisherman's ingenuity and patience for a spiritual catch. Fish do not come to our hand begging to be taken—nor do souls; and fishermen fish where they know there are fish. It does not need an angel from heaven to tell us to do likewise in soul winning.

The fisherman's heart is more important than his rod or his flies; the fish do not pay much attention to the amateur's fine equipment. Some trained psychologists have very little success in dealing with people because they do not really love them. All our good rules for soul winning will fall flat unless our hearts are aflame with love for souls.

Christ's voice is not the only one that calls us today. Ours is a noisy world, full of clamoring, conflicting voices: voices of pleasure, ambition, home, country, love, duty, war, death; voices of fear, of worry, of confusion. To what voice are you listening? Whom are you following? Is it a better voice than

His? a safer guide? a kinder master? Tune in to the station you really want to hear.

Close beside the Shepherd, we His joy may share.
He that winneth souls is wise.

Love Is Best

James 2:8-12; Col. 3:12-14; 1 Cor. 13:4-7

Put on the new man, which is renewed in knowledge after the image of him that created him (Col. 3:10).

Love is God's best. Lives of love will write into our characters lines of beauty and Christlikeness. And character is a value that God rates high. Given a new spirit, let us keep busy translating it into specific attitudes. I don't love out into space. That is sentimentality. I love people under specific—and usually trying—conditions. Love will work as I work.

1. I shall find it beautifully natural and happy to be unretaliative because I am no longer self-centered. I can see the other person's point of view, and I shall learn to look for it.

2. I shall not be eternally suspicious, because I am not worried about my own interests; I have given them to God to take care of. He can track down rumors better than I.

3. I shall not be itching for praise at the expense of others; I shall be glad for others to have their share. I love them as myself.

4. I shall be stirred, excited, thrilled over God's cause because my heart is centered there.

5. I shall look for the best in others, and find it. That is the nature of love.

37

Not automatic, not always easy; plenty of opportunities always to show some other spirit—but always the sense of fitness and naturalness. To love is normal, satisfying always.

By Thy wonderful power,
By Thy grace every hour,
Help me to love like Thee.

Adventuring with God

Heb. 11:8-12

Abraham believed God, and it was accounted to him for righteousness (Gal. 3:6).

Risk? or sound investment? No risk—for God has promised you His protection. You can live a charmed life until your work is done. For God himself will take care of your enemies.

If you hesitate to "give God all you don't know," you suggest that you are wiser than He—or kinder. In a world like ours I would rather shift the responsibility of life to stronger shoulders than mine!

God is still in the business of calling—and blessing. Many a young man would never have been heard of if he had not answered the call of God and gone out "from his father's house." To draw back from the call that is facing you today is to draw back from blessing.

Sometimes it is easier to say the big "Yes" in the initial leap of faith than to keep saying the small "yeses" along the way. Faith wears everyday clothes and proves herself in life's ordinary situations. In the way you answer or keep still today, in the tone of your voice or the curve of your lip, in your thoughts of confidence or self-pity you are "fight[ing] the good fight of faith"—or not.

And harder than to leave family and friends in a spectacular venture of faith is to live among them but not by their standards, walking life's ordinary paths but seeing God, mingling with the crowd but obeying higher standards. To risk the disapproval of your group is not easy; but it pays if it puts God on your side.

> *I gave God a lagging soul,*
> *Fast losing in the fight.*
> *He gave it back with chart and goal*
> *To climb the steeps of light.*
> —C. E. FLYNN

God Does Not Forget

Gen. 7:1-10, 23-24

The Lord is not slack concerning his promise (2 Pet. 3:9).

God does not forget His threatened judgments on evil. "It came to pass" (Gen. 7:10). Righteousness delivers—always. Sin pays off in death—always. In the end. And even now we are permitted sometimes to see God's mills grinding.

God does not forget His constant care of the good. "I have seen" (Gen. 7:1). "Where I really live enemies cannot come. . . . The strength of God is on the side of right. This inward certainty overwhelms my unknown future and I have no fears."—Samuel Young.

God does not forget definite directions for the obedient. "As the Lord commanded him" (Gen. 6:22; 7:5, 9). Always His the planning, mine the obeying. Easy to say, and easy to disregard when the plan includes details that seem too small to notice. A crack of a half inch could have sunk the ark.

One of the happiest things is to know that God really cares about the little details of my life today. He will help me in my minutes as well as in my days and years.

> *The storms will come, but fear not,*
> *For, Noah, I am nigh;*
> *And through the upper window*
> *You'll see Me standing by.*

The Comforter Has Come

Rom. 8:12-17, 26-27; Acts 4:31

But ye are not in the flesh, but in the Spirit, if so be that the Spirit of God dwell in you (Rom. 8:9).

The Spirit-filled Life. Watch the Spirit energizing a holy life. It becomes alive, dynamic, positive. The epochal experience is only the beginning; we prove our experience by developing a new Spirit-indwelt life. This means daily choice of the Spirit's leading until *spiritual habits* are built up. "We are debtors . . . to live after the [Spirit]."

We learn the necessity of keeping under the Spirit's *anointings.* We learn how out of weakness to become strong. There are still fearsome enemies to meet and still human shrinkings. But we learn that prayer will renew boldness, and we learn to pray things through. "We kneel, how weak! we rise, how full of power!"

We learn to let the Holy Spirit guide and control our *prayer life.* We stop asking for what we want, and begin to ask what He wants. We stop praying aimlessly and perfunctorily, and let Him teach us the effectual prayer. There is a grip in a Spirit-controlled prayer.

Spirit-filled Christians soon become *intercessors*. The Holy Spirit knows what it means for a soul to be lost, and He knows the worth of the blood of Christ. He fills our prayers with His own intensity.

> *Holy Spirit, all divine,*
> *Dwell within this heart of mine.*
> *Cast down every idol throne;*
> *Reign supreme, and reign alone.*

We Know Him

Luke 24:13-32

Did not our heart burn within us, while he talked with us by the way? (Luke 24:32).

Jesus makes himself known to individual hearts in a personal relationship. He comes to those who *talk of Him*. He will not force himself upon us. If we are too full of our own concerns to care, it is perfectly easy to live in Christian America as heathen, never even knowing there is a living Christ. "Indifference is our Public Enemy Number One."

We can *see Him*. Interested in Him, we find He is interested in us. We too can have Him walking by our side along life's dusty way, and all our common days can be a romance.

We can *talk to Him*. No worry is too petty to bring to Him, no problem too big. The extreme reverence which makes God so great that He cannot bother with our small affairs amounts to practical atheism.

We can *hear Him talk*. Much of our relationship with Jesus should consist of silence toward Him. What things He

41

will tell us: practical counsel for everyday matters, comfort for everyday sorrows, light for our eternities—as He makes the Bible a living book. Suppose I should miss all this by my chattering.

We can *entertain Him*. Let us not treat Jesus shabbily. We set before our other guests the best we have. "Give the best you have to the Best you know."

We can *eat with Him*—in daily communion. Communion is a rare art; but we need it sorely. Some part of our prayers must be more than asking, or we shall starve spiritually while going through the forms of prayer.

> *What a privilege to carry*
> *Everything to God in prayer.*

Jesus Interceding

John 17; Rom. 8:34

Father, I will that they also, whom thou hast given me, be with me where I am (John 17:24).

My Complete Savior. The hour of all the ages was the hour of Calvary. There Jesus gave His life to save me. But He did still more: He prayed for me. The Passion is steeped in intercession; the sacrifice is made efficacious by prayer. He took no chances with my soul.

Jesus prayed that I should be kept from the world's evil. Let me not fear the gathering power of unknown evil. His prayer will be a wall of fire about me.

He prayed that I should be sanctified wholly. I do not have to believe the doubters or the devil, who say the experience is not for me.

He prayed that I might be a good witness. He prayed that through my holy life others should believe in His power to save from sin. Though it seems to me that I do little for Him, I can spread His kingdom by living true today.

He prayed that His joy should be mine. He knows I need a song in my heart. Even today when life's disappointments are clutching at my heart and the whole world I have known is falling in ruins, His joy remains when all else goes.

He prayed that we should be one: the Father and the great body of sanctified believers and I. I am not solitary. I belong. Let me not cherish a suspicion nor raise a barrier between any fellow Christian and myself.

I am glad He prayed for me; I need to know He prays today. I will keep on believing in Him. His prayer is for those who believe.

He ever lives above For me to intercede,
His all-redeeming love, His precious blood to plead.

Vision Before Service

Isaiah 6

I saw also the Lord . . . high and lifted up (Isa. 6:1).

We need the vision. Is your prayer life so vital that it makes others hungry? Jesus' was; and He said we could follow Him.

These things that we see and handle every day are not the real, lasting things. How busy are we with them, how buried in them? Heavenly realities exist unnoticed, unseen; one day we shall stand face-to-face with them and be astonished—or confounded.

Heavenly realities exist, and some men see them. But they are picked men who appreciate God and spiritual things. And they prepare the way for the vision by waiting on God.

Our truest moments are those rare times when reality bursts through the veil and we see things in the light of eternity—shining clear through the mists of earth, sure and certain beyond all possibility of doubt. Just living will blur their distinctness and make them seem unreal. The cares of this life will choke our spiritual breath; we must fight sometimes as a drowning man would fight for air, to keep time for God to speak to us and make eternal reality seem real.

It is on intimate relationship with Jesus that we must ultimately rely for keeping. To abide in Him we must concentrate on Him.

> *Thou callest me to seek Thy face—*
> *'Tis all I wish to seek.*

Bought with a Price

1 Pet. 1:17-21

Ye were not redeemed with corruptible things, as silver and gold . . . but with the precious blood of Christ (1 Pet. 1:18-19).

Jesus came to die. His life finds its full meaning only in His death. Jesus' death was not accidental, not incidental. It was deeply and fundamentally essential. Calvary had to be. It had to be just as it was. For it has to be *right.*

God had not forgotten when He let Jesus go to the Cross. Nor was He arbitrary in His demand. He was planning in love and wisdom, planning the only way that would deal adequately with all the facts. Tragic, cruel, heartbreaking, impossible; but adequate—Christ the Lord of Glory crucified.

Sin must be dealt with; God could not overlook it. Calvary is adequate. Jesus' death proves the awful reality of sin. If you are tempted to dally with sin, or to wonder if the well-meaning sinner is really lost, take a look at Calvary. If sin is a light thing, why the Cross?

God must punish sin yet save man from it. His own Son, voluntarily paying the full penalty in man's place, set man free—justly, rightly, honorably, beautifully—and the personal relationship resulting eclipsed the evil of sin. "Where sin abounded, grace did much more abound." The Cross is God's answer to sin.

Has my sin been dealt with—through the Cross?

> *I am redeemed, but not with silver;*
> *I am bought, but not with gold;*
> *Bought with a price—the blood of Jesus,*
> *Precious price of love untold.*

The Cost of Discipleship

Matt. 19:22-26

But what things were gain to me, those I counted loss for Christ (Phil. 3:7).

It costs everything, but it is cheap at any price. Dr. J. B. Chapman, writing on "Cheap Religion," makes the point that you usually get what you pay for. If you don't want to pay much for your religion, you'll get a poor brand. Cheap religion is cheap. Salvation costs high; but it is a bargain at any price.

"The great refusal" is the refusal to enter into life. Anyone who turns from eternal life goes away "sorrowful"; he has made a poor bargain. He has exchanged eternity for time—and he never can make up his loss.

The price is your all; but He gives it back—that and more. And if you do not give it, it spoils on your hands. To keep a sweetheart you turn Jesus down, and the married life you build is likely to be bitter with heartache. To keep your money you turn from Jesus, but that money will never buy you satisfaction. Better give your treasures to Jesus; He knows just what will satisfy you. God never takes a thing from you but He gives you something better—it is good philosophy, and experience bears it out.

Christ knows the path to real greatness, and He will lead us in it. He knows the path is entered through self-surrender; and He will not cheat us by letting us think we can find it an easier way.

> *Oh, the Cross has wondrous glory!*
>   *Oft I've proved this to be true.*
> *When I'm in the way so narrow,*
>   *I can see a pathway through;*
> *And how sweetly Jesus whispers:*
>   *"Take the cross; thou need'st not fear,*
> *For I've trod the way before thee,*
>   *And the glory lingers near."*

The Cost of Discipleship

Matt. 19:27-30; Phil. 3:12-14

These are they which follow the Lamb whithersoever he goeth. These were redeemed from among men, being the firstfruits unto God and to the Lamb (Rev. 14:4).

Following Jesus—where will He lead? Self-surrender is only the door. On the other side, what? Not a blind alley with nothing beyond; not the edge of an abyss with the next step death. Surrender to Jesus is the first step of an endless adventure with Him.

The steps of this journey are readily traced. Count on every one: the wilderness of temptation, the mount of vision, the valley of service, the dazzle of passing popularity, the garden of intercession, the night of betrayal, the judgment hall of injustice, the cross—and the resurrection morning! Jesus knows well every step; He knows He is calling us to a rugged way. Yet He dares to insist, for He knows the glory of the end.

And the thrill of the journey itself. Who would live a torpid, indifferent, earthbound life when he might breast the winds and storm the stars? Following in His train, we know reality and achieve the triumphs that will ring through the ages.

> *Finding, following, keeping, struggling,*
>   *Is He sure to bless?*
> *Saints, apostles, prophets, martyrs*
>   *Answer, "Yes!"*

I Too Shall Live

1 Cor. 15:41-44

It is sown in corruption; it is raised in incorruption (1 Cor. 15:42).

Not buried, but sown. Those friends whom we have loved, those bodies so dear to us even after life has left them—we have not seen the last of them when they are put in the ground. They will spring up again, radiant, transformed, warm with life. The God who cares through the winter for the wheat seed sown in autumn will care for them till the resurrection spring morning.

It is when the dead hear the voice of Christ that they shall come forth from their graves. His is the quickening energy. It should not be hard for Christians to believe in the resurrection of the body. They have felt the stir of His eternal life in their souls.

Even here we may feel in our bodies the quickening energy of Christ—earnest of resurrection power. Test it next time you are "too tired to go to prayer meeting." Go, and find renewed freshness. Test it next time you face a day with no strength for its duties. Draw from Him "strength" as your "day."

In the resurrection, as in all else, we follow our Leader. As we have walked in His image, we shall be raised in His image. Jesus Christ had a natural body and a resurrection body; so shall we have. He took flesh, and He was glorified; so we. He is "the firstfruits"; we come after.

I shall be like Him, I shall be like Him,
And in His beauty shall shine.

If Jesus Had Not Come

Matt. 2:1-12

Whereby the dayspring from on high hath visited us (Luke 1:78).

If Jesus had not come, Christmas would only be "merry." Christmas gladness has its counterfeit in pagan reveling: drunkenness instead of the upward look, unrestraint for self-control, selfishness instead of goodwill. Jesus takes every human faculty and raises it to its highest level; He lifts life to its

48

best possibility; He gives the genuine of which anything else is only the counterfeit.

No Star of Hope. We are creatures of hope, but we cannot be creators of hope. Without a guiding star we lose our way. Jesus gives us a future. He pulls us out of the miry clay of our own failures and our own resources.

No finding shepherds, no worshiping Magi. All over the world from the beginning of time, human hearts have been seeking rest, human minds have been seeking truth. But there are no finders outside of Christ. Only in Him does the Spirit rest; only at His feet does the human heart worship in satisfaction.

No heavenly message, no word from God to man, no revelation of His goodwill. And I must grope in darkness as the heathen do, unsatisfied, sin-burdened, bewildered, lost. After 2,000 years are we keeping the message from them?

No good tidings, no gospel, no message for the lost, no testimony to saving grace. I must preach only law and no love. But:

> *We have heard the joyful sound:*
> *Jesus saves! Jesus saves!*
> *Spread the tidings all around:*
> *Jesus saves! Jesus saves!*

Life at Its Best

Eph. 4:11-20

Till we all come . . . unto the measure of the stature of the fulness of Christ (Eph. 4:13).

What have you set out to do with your life? You have only one to spend. What is your slogan? "Getting by"? "As good as the rest"? "Can't do that and be sanctified"? Or are you reaching out for "the measure of the stature of the fulness of Christ"? Let us all lift up our eyes, and stretch our souls, and look truth full in the face—truth and Jesus.

How much truth have we seen even in the past year? What possibilities of Christian strength and usefulness have we admitted? We shall need it all, for we have an infinite reach before us—an infinite reach and a glad goal: likeness to Him. "Recognized ideals are imperative."

Are the sails of my soul really set for the goal of Christlikeness? Or am I one of the crowd that drifts? Surely Jesus died to make us more than drifters or even merry-go-rounders.

When Jesus went to heaven He did not leave us orphans. He left us the Holy Spirit as His Executive. He is to guide us into all truth. He is to bear in our lives the fruit of Christlikeness.

Between the best moral life of good works and the humblest Christian life there is a great gulf fixed. The Christian life throughout is dependent on divine grace—that no flesh should glory. From first to last it is of the Spirit.

Oh, the unsearchable riches of Christ,
Wealth that can never be told!

2

Talks
to Young People

Your Slogan Makes a Difference

A tiny plaque in the office of the president's secretary caught my eye and my attention. It stayed with me. It challenged me and at the same time lifted me. Now that same motto is on the wall of my own office and has claimed not only my attention but my faith: "Not Somehow, but Triumphantly."

That slogan belongs not to me only; it belongs to every Christian, young or old. It is the legacy of Christ to us, the Christ who said as He went to the Cross, "In the world ye shall have tribulation: but be of good cheer; I have overcome the world." "My peace I give unto you."

Peace, that is it—His peace. Peace is not just a good feeling which we got at the altar and fear we may lose without knowing how or why. Peace is "the possession of adequate resources"—adequate resources for everything life can bring. It is the knowledge that with Christ we need not fail.

Let us start with the proposition that *Christians are not expected to muddle through*. They are expected to face life head-on and triumph. There is always a right way. There is *the* right way to meet every circumstance of life; and if we take the right way, we shall without fail be victorious in the long run, whatever the immediate outcome.

For a second proposition: *Life's difficulties are not watered down to fit our ability*. The problems are not given us already solved, nor even with answer appended. Christians are not spared troubles. They are thrown into a world of confused standards and irritating people and overwhelming temptations, and are told to live like Christians. . . .

So we come to our third proposition: *There is no need to be defeated*, or to live so sloppily or carelessly as to bring distress to ourselves or dishonor to the name of the Christ we serve. We must plan for a life that holds His banner high and walks a straight line onward—unashamed. It is no easy matter to trace a course through the confused, uncertain, contradictory maze of things and people that make up our world, but it is gloriously possible and simple.

For, a fourth proposition: *God will take us through if we will cooperate.* In every issue there is a right attitude that can be taken. At every turn there is a Voice saying: "This is the way, walk ye in it." We do not have to work out the strategy of victory for every situation. We have to choose once for all the will of God, get a sanctified heart, then commit ourselves to the principles of the Bible, in every questionable issue find the Christlike attitude to take, act accordingly—then let God do the rest. In other words, obey and trust.

It sounds simple. Too simple? Try it. Dare accept the challenge, and refuse to blunder, slide, and guess your life away. Dare accept God's definitions and God's solutions; and you have God's resources. "Not Somehow, but Triumphantly."

Trust Your Great Moments

Another slogan: "Trust Your Great Moments." Our world is full of shifting standards and ideas. Many conflicting voices are calling. The great moments of your life are those moments when through all the confusion God got a message through to you plain and certain. You saw things clear in eternity's light, the light of reality. The devil will try, or has tried, to blur your vision with dust and cloudiness; but if you will be honest with yourself, you know that in those moments you saw truth. You must hold to them as to your life; they are your life.

Go back to those moments. What did you see then? You had an Isaiah's great moment when you saw *yourself*. In the Temple at worship Isaiah saw himself: a sinner needing cleansing. Somewhere at worship—at camp meeting, at a revival service, by your own bedside—that vision came to you. You had heard holiness sermons before, but that time the Spirit showed you your own heart; and you saw that without His cleansing, your work for God would be in vain. And as you yielded your all in full consecration, you knew your nature was purged from sin. Hold fast to that moment. The enemy will fight it. Never let him persuade you that you can do God's work in your own strength or without the cleansing of the Blood.

You had a Peter's great Mount of Transfiguration moment when you saw *Jesus* and no man else. Everything besides faded from sight; you sang, "Take the world, but give me Jesus." You knew Christ was for you and for á lost world the Means of salvation, the Center of living, and the Touchstone of truth. You could test every thought and every act by Him. He was your Way, your Truth, your Life. Hold fast to that moment of insight. Never let anyone persuade you that anything better ever will be found. He is Alpha and Omega.

You had a Paul's great moment when you heard Christ's *commission* for your life. He laid hold upon you with such constraint that from that hour you were not your own; you were His. You knew your life was not useless. You had a never-ending job: to make known to others His saving and sanctifying power. You had something, Someone to live for; life had a meaning and a purpose. Hold fast to that moment, when the days seem drab and the routine presses. Look for the opportunity to turn someone from darkness to light. God will not waste your consecration.

You had a Moses' great mountain moment, when, like him, you were given *directions* for your lifework. "See . . . that thou make all things according to the pattern shewed thee in the mount." There is a specific plan for your life; don't be discouraged by circumstances into stopping short of it. Don't shrink yourself into a millionaire if God told you to become a missionary. And don't embroider a fancy career for yourself if He said, Witness where you are. Whatever He said, hold fast to His choice for you. It will prove the best.

Perhaps the moment that stands out clearest to you now is Elisha's, when he caught a glimpse of his departing teacher and was promised a double portion of his spirit to carry on his work; or John's on Patmos when he saw heaven and heard the song of the overcomers through the Blood. God still is revealing himself, even to us. Prize the moments of revelation; they are reality.

If we are to conquer, it will be by faith in our great moments. For they represent God's map of operations for us. He sees the whole.

Some Ordinary Day

Strange phrase for a slogan; yet I am trusting it will stay with you as it has stayed with me since it leaped out of a little poem I read months ago—leaped at me and became alive with meaning.

We are spending a year of ordinary days, 365 of them. Our lives are made up of ordinary days. Yet life is no ordinary thing. If we hold our ordinary days cheap—or count them common—we shall make an ordinary life. The word to Peter was, "What God hath cleansed, that call not thou common."

Every ordinary day given to God and touched by Him is a sacrament. And a life of God-blessed "ordinary days" can shake the world.

Ordinary days develop crises. It was an ordinary day of a Palestine summer when a mother's cherished son went out into the harvest fields with the reapers. Before noon he was brought back to her, dying of a sunstroke. Happy for that mother that she had been in the habit of entertaining the prophet of God on ordinary days! She knew where to find him, and his prayer restored her son to life. The preparation for the emergency is the habit of the ordinary.

Any ordinary day may be the day that God will choose to make extraordinary. "Trust Your Great Moments" [just noted] was one of our first slogans. The way to get great moments of call or commission or revelation is to keep the ordinary days open to God.

It was a very ordinary day in a tax collector's office. But the man at the desk was faithful and dependable and competent. Jesus came by and called, "Follow me"; and that day in Matthew's life became a red-letter day for him and for all who will read his Gospel as long as time lasts.

It was a very ordinary day on the farm; but God saw a young man doing a tedious job conscientiously as unto the Lord and selected Gideon for an exploit that was anything but ordinary. It was an ordinary day in the desert tending sheep—nothing could be less exciting; but Moses had a heart burdened with the need of his people, and he saw the bush burning with the presence of God. That ordinary day turned the world upside down.

Just an ordinary day with its ordinary "private devotions." It seems a simple routine. But suppose there had been no prayer time that day, with its opportunity for God to speak. Peter was on the housetop praying as his custom was, and God gave him the vision that opened the door for a

57

"whosoever will" preaching of salvation without respect of persons. Suppose he had not been there to receive it.

An ordinary testimony meeting—but Jesus came and stood in the midst of His disciples and said, "Peace be unto you." He says He will do that every time His followers meet, to the very end of the age. He does not plan for ordinary meetings.

An ordinary prayer meeting—the three had often gone apart with Christ. But this time on the mountain Moses and Elias were present, and Christ revealed His glory. Another ordinary prayer meeting, in the garden, so ordinary that they fell asleep. But this time their Lord was in sore need of their fellowship, and they failed—failed Him and failed themselves.

For the ordinary day can prove a day of sudden temptation. It did to Peter and James and John that night of Jesus' trial. When we face one ordinary day we cannot guess what it will hold for us. To be safe, we need every morning to ask in earnest, "Lead us not into temptation." Jesus was not playing with words when He gave us the prayer. Overpowering temptation comes unexpectedly and without warning—on an ordinary day.

It is on an ordinary day that the big opportunity comes, opportunity for success or failure. For a missed opportunity is a failure. The one difference between failure and success in life is keeping in touch daily, hourly, with God, by constant obedience. Then we shall not miss His appointments for us. With God there are no ordinary days.

Every ordinary day is precious beyond calculation. It might be the only one we shall have to give our Lord for love and service here before He comes. If we knew this ordinary day we are now beginning would be that last one, how careful we should be to live it for Him! "What I say unto you I say unto all, Watch," "lest coming suddenly he find you sleeping." Alert and loving then, these ordinary days.

No Worldliness

I heard someone in prayer the other day ask that God might help us to see actions as "black or white, not just gray," meaning, of course, that we might have clean-cut notions of right and wrong, stronger convictions, a keener sensitiveness to sin as sin. The prayer was a wise one. For the tragedy of our age is that we have lost this sense of sin. There is no clear line between sin and righteousness, between the world and the Christian.

Yet God from the beginning has made the dividing line very clear. His way has been the way of separation. Abel's offering was right; Cain's offering was wrong, dead wrong. The Israelites were God's children and were protected; Pharaoh's hosts were God's enemies and were drowned. Christ's disciples were to be "perfect, even as your Father which is in heaven"; the Pharisees were "of your father the devil." Jesus said, "Ye cannot serve God and mammon." He said men must leave all to follow Him. There is no halfway house, no middle ground, no no-man's-land. "If any man love the world, the love of the Father is not in him."

To be worldly is to live for time and sense rather than for eternity and God's program. "The world passeth away, and the lust thereof: but he that doeth the will of God abideth forever." If you care too much about what your group thinks, you can't care enough about what God thinks. If you follow the crowd, you can't follow Christ.

But where is the dividing line? What is "worldliness"? There are many ideas as to what makes a person worldly: almost as many ideas as there are religious groups—perhaps as many as there are individuals. Dress—or some item of dress. Amusements—or some type of amusement. And the person who frowns on the short skirt may wear the necklace; the person who won't attend the movies may listen to radio trash; the person who condemns dancing may indulge in necking—or vice versa. Until skeptics say, "It's all relative," "There are no fixed standards," "It's all in the way you were brought up."

They are wrong. There is spirituality, and there is worldliness; and there is a great gulf between. Worldliness has best been defined as "interest in things of time to the exclusion of things of eternity." "The lust of the flesh, and the lust of the eyes, and the pride of life." Any pursuit or attitude that makes God less than real in my life is to that extent worldly. Any activity is worldly that makes His presence less recognizable and His Spirit less dominant. A student or a businessman buried in his work can be as worldly as a society girl drowned in pleasure. It is not the name of the action but the nature of it that makes the wrong.

It is popular to decry negatives in religion. But the Christian must know how to say, "No." Some negatives are the condition for anything positive. I have to say an eternal "No" to Satan before I can say many "Yeses" to God. There are practices, diversions, and activities that will fill my mind with trash and stain it with filth; yet my God is holy, and I must be holy. At the entrance to the Christian life stands a great negative: "No" to the unholy and the unclean. And there are forms of entertainment that will fritter away time and energy that should be given to God and His service. The question is not only, "What harm is there in it?" Rather, "Does it keep me from something better?"

There are forms of amusement that the finest Christians of other days have found not conducive to the highest type of spirituality. And there are their successors of our day; different in name, but quite as dangerous rivals of God's program.

The principle is the same. I would take counsel with the best Christians I know rather than with the poorest samples of religion.

Worldliness is deeper than surface conduct. It expresses itself in conduct, but it is a thing of the spirit. The soul itself knows its worldliness; not even its friends are certain, though they can guess. It is a matter of the heart and its loves and its motives. Worldliness estranges the heart from God.

Millennia ago in a garden, God walked with a man and a woman. As long as they obeyed His "No," they enjoyed His fellowship, separated to Him and His love. As soon as they chose their own way and their own pleasure, they walked alone, separated from God. They had become worldly. They thought "it didn't make any difference." But it lost them God.

Only Beginnings

"There is no finality in this life, only beginnings."

The sentence is quoted from an editorial which stresses the New Year's opportunities for forgetting the past and going forward with life. But whatever the date, now is the time to remember that nothing you do is an end; every act, every thought, is a beginning.

> *Our echoes roll from soul to soul,*
> *And grow forever and forever.*

Everything you do sets in motion a current that will sweep on into eternity, piling up good or evil as it goes.

There is no finality of influence. "I didn't notice you were there, Jim"—apology for a careless oath and discomfort uttered one winter morning in the 1880s at McGill University, Montreal, where a few men practicing football were shivering in the cold—the words did not evaporate and die. They caught the attention of the young theological student James Naismith, to whom they were addressed, and stayed with him all his days as a sermon on his unconscious influence as a Christian. In addition they set him to thinking out a game which could be played indoors in cold weather, and so became the beginning of basketball, the most widely popular sport in the world.

Every word or deed, however casual, exerts an influence that goes on and on, gathering momentum until it bursts into eternity, then on and on through the ages.

To think too closely of the eventualities of influence would make one morbid in attitude and stilted in conduct. But to be careless of its beginnings is to throw away one's life. The only safe course is to commit our thoughts and words and doings to the guidance and control of the Holy Spirit, trusting Him to dictate our beginnings and overrule their working into good.

There is no finality set to work done. Everything you do in the name of Jesus and for His sake has eternity in it. It is a seed sown that will certainly bear fruit. It is a beginning of salvation for souls and building for the Kingdom. For God has promised to bless it. Unseen perhaps by men.

Enough that He heard it once:
We shall hear it by and by.

You are not seeing results? They will come if you are faithful. Prayers have been answered in glorious fulfillment long after the one who prayed was in his grave. Meantime, the example of your testimonies and consistent living and steady faith has caught fire in other lives.

There is no finality in failure—unless you will it. The disciples had toiled all night and had caught nothing. But Jesus said, "Cast the net on the [other] side." And they drew it to land full of fishes. Every day you may have a direct suggestion from the Spirit as to His thought for your plan of action that day; every day may open a channel of blessing into some life, or lay the foundation for some Kingdom enterprise. The years will carry it on to start you out in eternity with a wealth of capital. . . .

There is no finality set to "ordinary" Christian living. Today by your faithfulness to duty you are beginning a solid foundation for obedience to the will of God that Satan cannot overturn in the day of crucial test that is ahead. Today by your regular attendance at Sunday School and church services you are beginning a Christian character that will not crumble into worldliness and self-indulgence when the subtle temptations of busy, care-beset middle age comes on. Today by your quiet refusal to listen to an unkind story you are beginning a personality of beauty and an atmosphere of blessing that will spread love and healing wherever you go. Today by teaching a group of children you may be beginning a church in Africa or India. Today by your regular keeping of your devotional hour you are beginning an everlasting friendship with God. Today by patient continuance in well-doing you are beginning heaven for yourself and others. These are all gracious things; but they must have beginnings.

There is no finality of despair; hope always can begin afresh. The Christian hope is an anchor that steadfastly holds within the veil. Worry is barren; hope is productive. So worry is ruled out: the door to the past we close, for just ahead is the future's door—wide open. There is no dead-end street for the true wayfaring Christian. . . .

Life is not a few blank years and months; life is the beginning of eternity.

One Life

"We are all under sentence of death with an indefinite reprieve." So writes Walter Pater. It seems that Rousseau, upon learning that he was smitten with an incurable disease, asked himself how he could make the utmost use of the interval of life that remained. (He decided for the intellectual stimulus of reading a clever writer!)

But Peter makes the point that the one thing certain for all of us is that we shall die. Only a counted number of heartbeats remain to any of us, old or young—counted by God. How shall we invest those heartbeats? Peter urges us to get as many pulsations as possible into our days, not to lose those days by indifference. Don't be listless, he says, but awake. Feel the richness of life. Fill it with vital experience.

Fine—and true, we all agree. The question is, what sort of experience? Your answer depends upon what life is to you, and what you want to make of it.

The author of the Persian *Rubaiyat* said, Life is a *Tavern* and we'll have a good time: "Come, fill the cup."

> *The Bird of Time has but a little way*
> *To flutter—and the bird is on the wing.*

Many young people are viewing life, and living it, with that same don't-care spirit:

> *Ah, take the Cash, and let the Credit go,*
> *Nor heed the rumble of a distant Drum.*

Enjoy yourself today, whatever may happen tomorrow.

Robert Louis Stevenson, for years half dead of tuberculosis and always facing imminent death, saw life as a *Race* in a wilderness of snares and pitfalls. But he came of a family of lighthouse engineers whose creed was sound workmanship, and he counseled, "Stop your ears against paralyzing terror, and run the race with a single mind. Begin some work even if you have only a week to live. Courage! *Do* something, and do it well. Don't fold up, useless. You were made for action."

Robert Browning, in *Rabbi ben Ezra*, says life is a *Potter's Wheel*. We are the clay and our life has a purpose. Every day, every circumstance counts in fashioning us into a cup for the Master's use in eternity. We are not our own. Our highest privilege is to choose the will of God and know that he is making out of our raw material something which He can use and enjoy.

Three very different views of life.

What you see as the meaning of life determines the use you put it to. It does not take long to show up. One year I told each of our college seniors how he was looking at life. Would you like to glimpse down some of those vistas with me? Each view shows us an angle of the entire beautiful truth about life.

Life is an *Inn*. I will not live as if I planned to stay here always. I will not change the cut of my heavenly clothes to suit the fashions of an overnight lodging.

Life is a *Prelude* to the vast symphony of eternity. Life is a *Rehearsal* for the performance of heaven. What I do in my Today is not detached; it has a direct bearing on my Forever.

Life is not easy. Life is a *Battle*. But I shall not lie down nor run away. For the issues are vast and victory is possible.

Life is a *Lesson*. I cannot understand it all at once, but if I persevere I shall look back from the last page and read its meaning complete and glorious.

Life is a single *Arrow* that I must shoot. Tragic if I shoot at random. I must choose a mark and practice my aim. Life is a *Ladder*, up or down. I must place it erect, found it sure, and brace it firmly.

Life is a *Heritage* handed down to me from those who have gone before. I have great privileges; I must show my gratitude by making the most of my legacy.

Life is a *Torch.* I must pass on undimmed to those who shall come after me the light that shines on my way; every privilege is a responsibility.

Life is a *Book* I am writing to be read by those about me and by those who will come after me. It still has blank pages, but I shall fill them all; and once I have written, I have written.

Life is a *Loom* where I am weaving a garment of praise or of dishonor. Every action, every thought, goes into woof and web; none is too trivial. For life is a *bundle* of little things.

Life passes so swiftly, so silently that it would trick us into thinking it does not matter. But it matters infinitely. For life is a *Loan* from God to us, a loan to be repaid with interest. Life is God's great *Investment*—your life and mine. I will not disappoint Him.

Life is a *Mission* upon which He has sent me with work to do for Him. We cannot do it alone, but we need not. For life can be a *Flame,* the flame of the love of Christ in our hearts, ever burning but never burning out.

Only one life—to live is Christ!

Life's Answers

We hear a great deal today about life's problems and life's questions. I would counter with life's answers. I hear these in the echoing, chanting, pulsating rhythm of Paul's declaration of faith: "And now abideth faith, hope, [love], these three." Here is the *summum bonum.* Here are the Christian's three answers to life's three tests. The tests do not change from age to age, nor—thank God—the answers. They abide.

"Now abideth faith"—in Christ. We *want to depend* on people and on familiar situations. But life takes the props from under every one of us; this is part of growing up. A person becomes a man when he learns that he cannot lean; he must stand alone. The teaching process is more or less gradual; but sooner or later slow motion changes to quick; in some devastating experience life is torn up by the roots or goes to pieces under us. Then,

> *When all around my soul gives way,*
> *He then is all my Hope and Stay—*

if we have learned to trust Him. At any rate, He is there. Faith is pure when all else is gone; faith is proved by obedience through the fog and the darkness. "He that believeth on me . . ." Christ will not let you down. Faith abideth.

"Abideth . . . hope"—in Christ. *We want to see ahead.* But life is full of blind alleys. Sooner or later we shall run into one: a situation that is impossible, a tangle that is insoluble, a mess that we have caused ourselves, a failure that is unforgivable. What then? Discouragement? fear? despair? Turn fatalist? A person becomes a man when he learns to face failure: he has fallen down; he must get up.

There is hope for the hopeless. Faith in God, therefore hope. "The God of hope" is named Providence. Never say, nor think, "Fate is against me." God is for you. Let Him show you the way out; let Him make your plans. Because Christ has died and risen and gone to heaven, interceding for us, bearing our names written on His hand, no situation is hopeless. Our hope is anchored in Him. There is no dead end for the Christian who will not let go of Christ; Satan cannot tear you out of the plan of God. There always is hope—in Christ.

"Abideth . . . love"—in Christ. The greatest of all, for Christ *is* love. *We want to succeed.* And Life says, Shift for yourself; no one else is going to look out for you. But a person becomes a man when he learns what real success is and how to find it. Love says, Forget yourself, and look out for others to help as well as yourself. Live as Christ lived; He was the great Success. And the love of Christ enables you to live by love.

Love is positive, not negative. It is a dynamic, driving urge. It gives you more than the Stoic's "Grin and bear it" to meet life with. It gives you the Kingdom to put first and a world of people to bless with Christ's Golden Rule. Love is omnipotent. In saving and blessing others you save and bless yourself. Try it. Try loving your enemy and pushing your rival's interest. "Abideth . . . love"—in Christ.

They say the world is going to pieces around us. It looks that way. But in the most stirring shipwreck story of all time Paul proved his own philosophy. He held to faith and hope and love. "I believe God"; "Be of good cheer"; "There shall be no loss of any man's life." "They escaped all safe to land."

The answer for all life's unknowns and uncertainties: "Abideth faith, hope, love."

"Such as I Have"

"Silver and gold have I none; but such as I have give I thee." When Peter (at the gate of the Temple) made this reply to the lame man who had asked for money, he was not speaking apologetically. He spoke confidently, with the glow of promise and expectation. He knew he was giving the cripple something far better than alms for a day.

"Such as I have"—what was it? Rather, who was it? It was Jesus, Master of human needs. And what made Peter so sure? He knew Him in the experiences of life. "No more Simon, but Peter"—Changer of weak natures to strong. "Follow me"—Giver of direction and goal to life. "Peace, be still"—Master of storms. "Bid me come to thee on the water"—Empowerer for impossible undertakings. "Lazarus, come forth"—Healer, Life-Giver. "Give ye them to eat"—Feeder of the hungry. "Feed my sheep"—Forgiver of failure and faithlessness.

How did Peter know him? "By promises fulfilled and words translated into life. The promise "I will rise" translated into Easter morning proved Him Victor. "Tarry," "I will send . . . the Comforter" translated into Pentecost proved Him Giver of spiritual power. "The Spirit . . . shall testify of me" translated into daily guidance proved Him living Companion and Friend, more real even than when He walked on earth.

"Such as I have"—the knowledge of Jesus Christ has enriched me too. I too have been granted this wealth to share with others. I say it to His praise. I too have known Him as Transformer of shifty nature, Stiller of storms, Helper of weak attempts, Supplier of bread and daily strength. I too have failed Him and been trusted again. I too have felt His resurrection life; I too have tarried and received the Spirit; I too have been taught by Him day by day. I too would share my experience of Jesus. I would say to every crippled soul I meet, "Such as I have give I." Every one in all the world has the same basic needs. He will never disappoint one, for He satisfied me.

How have I known Him? As Savior first, from sins realized and unrealized, from deceit, from selfish ambition, from laziness and unwillingness. The sight of His cross showed me my treacherous nature; His word changed my quicksand, too, to rock.

I too have known Him as Counselor. Without Him I should have been bewildered and lost in a confused world. But He directed my basic choices; at every turn I heard His

"Follow Me." And looking back, I see the way He led me was good.

How do I know Him? As faithful Guide He has given meaning to my life; He has given me a cause to live for that is bigger than I am. The very day I gave myself wholly to Him, He gave me a work to do for Him. Delivering me from an almost certain death, He laid claim to my service for life. At every crossroads the word of direction has come in the nick of time. In the keenest temptation to think myself a useless failure, He has repeated, "I have chosen you . . . that ye should go and bring forth fruit, and that your fruit should remain."

How do I know Him? I have come to know Him as Provider and Giver of bread. I have found my specific tests that if I would give daringly to the Kingdom He would fill up the lack in my purse; if I would "rest in the Lord" He would care for my interests.

How do I know Him? As Master and Teacher. He taught me with the basin and towel that my work was to be done selflessly for Him: "Seekest thou great things for thyself? Seek them not." He taught me that things—rewards and material possessions—do not matter so much: "I am your Possession." He taught me to pray, "Establish Thou the work of my hands," and promised—but how can I tell all my secrets?

How do I know Him? As Friend, Comforter, Strengthener, with me always. In my early teens He took my mother but whispered in my ear a word of comfort I had not known was in the Bible: "They shall see his face; and his name shall be in their foreheads." And in every emergency since He has been there to speak the lifting word. How faithfully those words have come! Alone under the wreckage of a railroad car, "Jesus, every day the same." At the point of crucial test, "Lo, a spring of joy I see." In heavy loss, "God hath provided some better thing." Battling weakness and illness, the healing word, "All things are possible to [her] that believeth." Fighting for a soul when it seemed too late: "Even now"; and again, "The faith of the Son of God."

"Such as I have"—it is worth recommending, recommending with a shout!

Faith in Christ is not an upside-down cone teetering tipsily on its point; faith in Christ is a pyramid resting firmly on its base, broadening down and settling surely so that it cannot be overturned, more real and more precious than life. It is "better farther on." . . .

"Such as I have"—"give"! I would be a Peter to give Jesus to the needy. I would be an Andrew to recommend Him and introduce Him boldly and confidently.

3

On a Christian Classic

I

The Tricks of Satan

Theology Made Practical

Two of the "must" books in English literature are Christian classics that appeared originally within seven years of each other—Puritan classics. They are *Paradise Lost,* by John Milton, and *Pilgrim's Progress,* by John Bunyan. The one has been called "an epic of the human race"—intellectual, artistic, sublime; the other might be called "The Plain Man's Pathway to Heaven"—practical, colloquial, down to earth. But both have lived now for almost 300 years and are more highly regarded today than when they were written. They have something that is larger than Puritanism, fine as that movement was—something as large as the heart of man the world over, deep as his need of God.

Puritanism is often misunderstood. The Puritans are thought of as more or less hypocritical, self-righteous 17th-century killjoys who tried to regulate other people's lives by their unreasonable prejudices. "Dost thou think because thou art virtuous there shall be no more cakes and ale?" It is a false picture. The Puritan did feel a responsibility for his neighbor's soul because he himself took salvation seriously. But Puritanism is not a 17th-century sect; Puritanism is a spirit that persists in every age, the spirit of Protestant Christianity. To the Puritan there are three real personalities in the universe: God and I, and the devil; the sinner and his Savior, and the tempter. All else is, in comparison, unimportant. Man has fallen, but there is salvation for him: complete justification by faith in Christ. Man is free in will and in action, and the devil is active; hence temptation, and hence probation. As long as one lives it is possible to fall—possible, but not necessary.

These are the doctrines of Puritanism; its spirit is vital, intense. God is real and life cannot be ordinary. At home with unseen realities, the Puritan in a lax, worldly age believed that a personal God and a personal devil are warring for every individual soul. Life is a struggle, a drama, a battle between good and evil; the battleground is the human soul; and every man takes sides. So action is emphasized. What to *do?* No one can be passive. Everyone must choose one side or the other.

These two great spokesmen, then, emphasize choice: right action in the light of personal accountability to God. The central theme of *Pilgrim's Progress* and *Paradise Lost* is temptation and the way to victory.

Milton is a theologian: Puritan plus scholar plus artist. In glorious word-music and lofty pictures he narrates the story of the fall of man and the promised redemption. His purpose is theological: to "justify the ways of God to man." *Paradise Lost* is the source of many of our ideas that we think we got from the Bible. And it "centers in the apple"; that is, in the temptation of man.

You remember the story: war in heaven; Satan, cast out, rallies his forces in hell, and decides to achieve revenge on God by tempting the newly created Adam. God foresees this: in a council in heaven Christ offers himself as a Savior, and an archangel is sent to warn Adam. Satan tempts; and Eve eats first, then Adam follows suit. The pair are driven from the garden, but first they hear from the archangel the prophecy of redemption.

Note the doctrines. (1) Satan: a subtle, powerful adversary—cruel, relentless, self-willed, determined, untiring, clever. (2) God: omniscient and just, all-wise and all-good. He foreknew sin, but He was just and loving; for He warned Adam, and He provided salvation through Christ. There

76

is still a mystery of evil, but God is justified. (3) Adam: free to will and to choose between obedience and disobedience.

The nature and effect of sin are studied in the personality and history of Satan himself. Its beginning was in the ambition or self-centeredness of Satan. (Sin, in Milton's "Allegory of Sin and Death," sprang full-grown from the forehead of Satan one day in heaven when Christ was publicly exalted.) Satan deteriorates by his own positive choice. At first an "archangel ruined," he chooses not to repent but to seek revenge on God, his sole interest rebellion against God's will. From the moment that he says, "Evil, be thou my good," and commits himself irrevocably to evil, he steadily grows uglier.

Paradise was "lost" when Adam yielded to temptation; it will be "regained" when the second Adam does not yield but resists Satan.

This is the systematic theology of Milton—not all Bible, but amplifying the Bible and so true to the spirit of the Bible that many of us scarcely know where the Bible stops and Milton begins.

* * *

Milton is theologian, we have said. Bunyan is preacher, evangelist, pastor. He has the same Puritan intensity, the same passion for the Word of God, the same keen vision of the things that are not seen; but he has with these a practical interest in everyday living. With him theology must be put to work; she must put on ordinary clothes and prove her strength. Out of his own experience he writes to give practical help to those who must meet temptation. Milton outlines the situation and states the problem; Bunyan gives the actual tryout. Milton shows us behind the scenes the devil and his forces, reveals their strategy and their plan of campaign; Bunyan gives the actual engagement on the stage of life. Milton shows us the boundless faith of the Son of God for the redemption of the wayward human race; Bunyan shows us the lonely pilgrim on his way. Milton sketches the plan of atonement; Bunyan shows the burden falling off at the Cross and rolling into the sepulcher. The same theology, here made concrete.

And because this work is not the narrow creed of a sect but the heart of the Bible embodied imaginatively, *Pilgrim's Progress* is broadly human, universal. It has been translated into practically all languages; it is written in the idiom of life, so quotable and is quoted constantly. More than that, it is translatable—and is translated constantly—into life, your life and mine.

"Not Ignorant of His Devices"

Bunyan wrote 60 works in all—4 of them great works: *Grace Abounding,* his spiritual autobiography; *The Life and Death of Mr. Badman,* a spiritual biography; *The Holy War* and *Pilgrim's Progress,* spiritual allegories. All are spiritual, all full of his own experience, all variations on this theme of temptation and resultant victory or defeat: God and the devil contending for the soul of man, and man casting the deciding vote.

In our consideration of *Pilgrim's Progress,* then, our first study will be of the variety of temptation: "The Tricks of Satan," or the devices he uses in his battle with man. *Pilgrim's Progress* is allegory made real by observation and experience. It is full of pictures of temptations—and defeats or victories —in actual life. (Almost every situation has its parallel in *Grace Abounding.*) The devil appears in various shapes: as Apollyon, the fierce destroyer who fights in the open; as Giant Despair, who lures the unwary traveler into his "stinking dungeon"; as Prince Beelzebub, who shoots his arrows of doubt at the man who begins to pray, that same Beelzebub who with Apollyon and Legion is proprietor of Vanity Fair and persecutor of pilgrims. The devil is shown in action. Temptation is presented in all the complexity of real life—a much more subtle thing than the simple fact of *Paradise Lost* or of our formal theology.

Mr. Valiant-for-Truth's list will serve as a good summary. (Part I of *Pilgrim's Progress* has recounted the journey of Christian from the City of Destruction to the Celestial City. Part II tells of his wife Christina's trip later with her children over the same route. Near the end of the journey this second group meets a pilgrim, Mr. Valiant-for-Truth, who narrates his experiences in the way.) He tells how his friends had tried to scare him out of starting on pilgrimage. "They told me that it was the most dangerous way in the world, that which the pilgrims go." (You can live very comfortably without temptation if you never start the Christian life—if you are willing to remain in the City of Destruction or in Dark-land, Valiant-for-Truth's old home.)

$$* \quad * \quad *$$

But temptation does not always come because the way is too hard. More subtle and dangerous are the temptations of ease.

$$* \quad * \quad *$$

Not all Christians have identical temptations. The exact shapes these take vary according to the different temperaments of the individuals. . . . The point we are emphasizing here is the versatility of the tempter, the subtlety of his appeals, the cleverness of his disguises.

II

The Means of Grace

For clear-cut teaching of the doctrine of conversion and the development of a consistent, godly Christian life we should go far to find another work as clear as Bunyan's in *Pilgrim's Progress*. The author writes out of a definite and rich personal experience. He gives us theology made alive by concrete examples and symbols. What he does for temptation he does for the means of grace; he draws living, unforgettable pictures. How build a Christian life? How make progress in the way to heaven? Here is a clear, trustworthy road map ("note of directions," he would call it). We can well afford to take time out to do as he advised his pilgrims to do: look into it, check our course by it, and direct our steps accordingly.

*   *   *

The sinner is saved by faith, not by feeling. Once in the way, once the recipient of divine grace, it is no concern of the Christian when or how the assurance of salvation, the "witness of the Spirit," reaches him. When "thou comest to the place of deliverance" the burden "will fall from thy back of itself." (Here Bunyan is true to his own experience. In *Grace Abounding* he narrates his own terrific struggles with doubt before assurance and inner peace sweep through his soul.) And sure enough, as Christian runs up the pathway—runs, notice, though still encumbered with his burden—he comes to a cross on a little hill, and below it a sepulcher. "So I saw, in my dream, that just as Christian came up with the cross, his burden loosed from off his shoulders, and fell from off his back, and began to tumble, and so continued to do so, till it came to the mouth of the sepulchre, where it fell in, and I saw it no more."

This is the secret of assurance, the sight of the Cross, the realization that "He died for *me*." I am saved by His death. My sins are buried with Him.

*   *   *

The Christian must learn the lesson of God's keeping power. Christian sees the fire burning hotter, in spite of the fact that a man continually pours on water to quench it. Astonishing! But on the other side of the wall another man is pouring secretly a continuous stream of oil into the fire. No wonder it does not go out. Impossible as the temptation seems to endure, we need not fear that the world, the flesh, or the devil can put out our fire so long as Christ pours on the oil of His grace. If we can early get into our systems "My grace is sufficient for thee," we shall be spared much suffering and perhaps some falls.

These standards once established, these and others taught in symbol at the Interpreter's House—as trust in grace, not works; careful obedience to light; readiness for the coming judgment—these standards of belief established at the outset, the Christian life will be steady and sure, based on the Word of God, which liveth and abideth forever.

The Palace Beautiful and the Delectable Mountains

The right start, the right standards—a sound conversion and Bible standards; now growth in grace. And strange to say, we grow by life's trials. "I cannot praise," said Milton, "a fugitive and cloistered virtue that never sees her adversary." Nor does God. He knows we must be tried, to be refined. He knows we must wrestle, to develop muscle. And we must remember that the devil's temptation is God's testing—

testing and developing. Every testing bravely and faithfully endured is followed by a special blessing or achievement. At the top of the Hill Difficulty come the peace and strengthening of the Palace Beautiful. In the Valley of Humiliation after the fight with Apollyon, Christian is refreshed with heavenly bread and wine, and his wounds are healed with leaves from the tree of life. And from the persecution of Vanity Fair he comes out a soul winner, having won Hopeful by his steadfastness.

Of the means of grace the Church is the great depository and dispenser. A Christian is weak who tries to live and walk alone. There is strength in Christian fellowship; more than that, the greatest blessings come by way of Christian fellowship. Jesus founded the Church and set His disciples in the Church. Soon after the Cross comes the "very stately palace, whose name is Beautiful." It stands close by the highway and was "built by the Lord of the hill, for the relief and security of the pilgrims." This is the Church.

✳   ✳   ✳

Throughout the book Bunyan lays stress on the benefits and responsibilities of Christian fellowship. Christian, Faithful, and Hopeful help one another. Where one is weak, another is strong; where one would falter, another warns and encourages. We help ourselves on to heaven as we help one another. By sharing experiences and declaring our faith one to another we encourage ourselves in the Lord. I wonder if we do enough of this in these days. The promise was, too, that the Lord would hearken and hear, and write the book of remembrance.

III

Real Life and Real People

Real as is the physical setting to us—Macaulay says "this is the highest miracle of genius, that . . . the imaginations of one mind should become the personal recollections of another"—the persons of the allegory and the life they live are just as real. In spite of their telltale names, sometimes even because of those names—Honest, By-Ends, Hopeful, and the rest—they are not allegorical abstractions. Uninteresting, for example, as the name Mr. Money-Love sounds, we find the person himself to be a brisk businessman whom we should recognize anywhere. The characters are actual men and women, no two repeating each other, as do not two of God's creation. Characters superficially so like as Little-Faith, Fearing, and Feeble-Mind are differentiated. A simple phrase may call forth a personality; as, the "young woman whose name was Dull." Speeches so short as those of the Vanity Fair jury, though obviously fitted to the speaker's names, call up in our minds without the slightest mental exertion real men, all harsh and intolerant, but each himself. Mr. Honest gives the clue when he says his name is "not Honesty in the abstract." So Bunyan thought of his characters. They were real to him, vivid in his own thought and imagination. They had walked into his book out of real life. How often he says, "I saw."

But what has all this to do with Christians and the Christian's job? This, at least. Our gospel must find people where they are; it must work with people as they are. *Pilgrim's Progress* has been recognized universally as true; it is good for us to become acquainted with every person and every situation. The knowledge will help us in our quest for paths to the hearts of men.

*   *   *

Bunyan is triumphantly optimistic—not about human nature, but about human nature plus God. He has small hope in the native goodness of man, but he has an unflinching confidence in the Word and power of an ever-present God.

IV

Thinking the Bible in Pictures

Bible Sources

What has made Bunyan's images so compelling and so lasting is the double fact that they are (1) true to human nature . . . and (2) based upon the Bible. Bunyan uses a few images that cannot be traced to the Bible as their original. He was saturated with Scripture metaphor; his method is to take a verse that implies a comparison, draw the implied image, and so compel the reader to look straight at it and realize its full meaning.

In this connection we may note the different effect produced by the symbols of Bunyan and of Dante, the great medieval poet. Dante's master work, *The Divine Comedy,* is splendidly allegorical; but the symbols do not grip us immediately as do Bunyan's. For they are based on scholastic logic and reasoned theology rather than on the Word of God, which we know and love, and which fits human nature as the glove fits the hand.

The Bible furnishes the germ of the allegory. "Here we have no continuing city, but we seek one to come." "Strangers and pilgrims." "Enter ye in at the strait gate." Put these three texts together, and you have *Pilgrim's Progress* in embryo. Bunyan does something to this germ. (Similarly *The Holy War* carries out in detail the scriptural figure of the Christian life as a warfare.)

The clearest allegorical incidents and situations are transferred directly from biblical images: the man in rags ("All our righteousnesses are as filthy rags"—Isa. 64:6); the Wicket Gate ("I am the door," "Strait [narrow] is the gate"); Hypocrisy climbing over the wall ("He that . . . climbeth up some other way"); "the valley of the Shadow of Death" (but see what the imagination of Bunyan has added); Beulah ("For the Lord delighteth in thee, and thy land shall be married"—Isa. 62:4); the City itself—just a word and a phrase, and Bunyan's creative power has done the rest. The most trivial details will be discovered to be realistic adaptations of some biblical phrase which we have never noticed particularly. . . . It is the Bible and human nature wedded. And for this reason its symbols have lived.

4

More Devotionals

I Can Be Sure

John 1:1-13

In him was life; and the life was the light of men (John 1:4).

I need to be sure. I have a unique, irreplaceable treasure, one life. I do not fully understand it, but its very mystery tells me I should not be careless with it. If I should make an error, I have no second life.

Is there any way of being certain what beliefs to adopt as controlling standards, what outlines of conduct, what directions of goal and purposes? I know I must eat and sleep and pay my taxes—but there must be a larger why and what. I live in a world that seems to be adrift. Most of the people are guessing their way through. Can I know and act positively?

I can be certain. The Giver of my life himself came to earth; spoke in distinct, clear words; gave the directions for successful maximum living; then lived a pattern life. He promised that if I would plan my conduct as He said, He would see to it that I should have the ability to succeed. Nothing could be plainer than this, nothing more dependable.

It will be a comfort to get back to first principles. The din of conflicting voices has a way of confusing even those who thought they knew. Just how am I to build up a life that has gone to pieces? Just how to strike anchor if I find myself adrift? The answer: Take a steady look at Jesus and hear what He has to say.

His revelation will prove itself genuine to the wide-open heart. As the curator of the great art museum said to some

89

unappreciative tourists, "Our pictures are no longer on trial—our visitors are."

> *I prayed for One to take my hand*
> *And guide me every day.*
> *Then I met Jesus.*

Only One Life

1 Pet. 1:23-25; Eccles. 12:1-7, 13-14

So teach us to number our days, that we may apply our hearts unto wisdom (Ps. 90:12).

Life—Planned or Unplanned? Jesus rang the changes on it because, though it is always staring us in the face, it is so easy to forget: Only one life, what shall we do with it? What are we doing with it?

Many, many people—most people—live haphazardly as the days come. They eddy about with their group, pushed by their impulses, on a slower or a higher level but still drifting: eating, sleeping; eating, sleeping, loving, movies, cards; eating, sleeping, dressing, going, seeing; money-making, money-spending; reading and studying, reading and studying; even churchgoing and social service done mechanically, without a vision. God made us to look up—why live like moles?

Everyone should aim to make some contribution to his generation before he passes on. Life should not disappear like a bubble leaving no trace. Whether your name is known or not, you want to leave an influence for good. You want flowers of blessing to spring up wherever your steps have gone.

The highest word the Old Testament has for a way of living is "wisdom." "So teach us to [order] our days, that we may [get us a heart of] wisdom." Wisdom is planning a life in the will of God.

The New Testament echoes, "Present your bodies a living sacrifice . . . that ye may prove . . . [the] perfect will of God."

Living for Jesus through earth's little while,
My dearest treasure the light of His smile.

Only One Life

Luke 12:31-34; Titus 2:11-14

But seek ye first the kingdom of God, and his righteousness; and all these things shall be added unto you (Matt. 6:33).

The Great Investment. You forsake all; you take the cross. The cross is Jesus' way of life, and of death. You invest once for all in the riches of heaven; you keep reinvesting. And the account accumulates.

Invest in prayer, and you will meet souls saved in heaven. Prayer costs, but the souls you buy are worth more than the time and strength you spend—how much more you will learn someday. Invest in sacrifice. Offer to God what costs you something—time, talents, hands, feet, voice, money—and feel the glow of His approbation. Invest in Christlikeness. Be generous, forgiving, kind, thoughtful, compassionate, even when it would be easy to think of self. Invest in soul saving. Go to church to lift, teach a Sunday School class, do personal work, testify in prayer meeting and outside. Sow beside all waters. You are not working for pay, but the treasure is piling up.

Being rich toward God is good judgment from every point of view. The self-life was temporary and shortsighted; this new life bears fruit that will multiply forever. The self-life was deceitful; this is a sound investment vouched for by the blood of the Son of God and tested by multitudes of redeemed souls. The self-life was impure and unholy; this purges and renews life to the core and fills with holy love. The self-life was lonely and isolated; this makes one a sharer of hopes and prospects and interests with all God's people, a member of the fellowship of the saints and the household of faith, never again to be a solitary.

> *Oh, the joy when I shall wake*
> *Within the palace of the King!*

Laws of the Kingdom

Matt. 5:1-12

The kingdom of God is . . . righteousness (Rom. 14:17).

The Mind of Christ. You are not compelled to be a Christian; you have a perfect right to steer clear of Jesus Christ if you choose. But once you take His name, you are obligated to live by an altogether different program from other people. Or you are living under false pretenses; your name of Christian is a living lie.

Jesus' use of the word *kingdom* is deliberate and significant. We do not drift haphazardly to heaven. There are definite and distinctive laws, binding upon all who call themselves citizens and imperative for all who expect to enjoy benefits and rewards.

The laws of the Kingdom are inflexible, but they are not arbitrary. They are based in the character of the King. "Let this mind be in you, which was also in Christ Jesus." Read the Beatitudes and you see Jesus' portrait.

The basic standards of the Kingdom are not stated as commands or obligations; rather, as "blesseds" or privileges. This is the genius of the Kingdom. God himself will not force you to be Christlike. He will open your eyes to see the superiority of Jesus' way; He will make you everlastingly dissatisfied with anything cheaper. And, in comparison, everything else will seem cheap.

"Strength where it ought to be—within" (a great educator's requisite for success in study). The glory of the Kingdom standard is that it embodies itself in an invincible spirit imparted to those who will receive it. There is no moral cave-in for the man whose heart has been captured by the King.

You must kneel at His feet
If you'd look on His face.

Singing unto the Lord

Psalm 146

Sing unto the Lord a new song, and his praise from the end of the earth (Isa. 42:10).

Why the Book of Psalms? Why a hymnbook at the heart of our Bible? Because God's salvation goes so deep. When the depths of our natures are stirred, we must express our emotion. And song is its natural voice.

We were made to sing. Some of us have defective machinery for producing it, but all of us respond to harmony; and we thrill when others express the beauty of sound and thought which we feel but cannot utter. The Book of Psalms gives us all an outlet. Every psalm sings a song that at one time or another we shall need as our own.

Sincere emotion is the mark of the song that lives. So the psalms will never die; for in them human experience is suffused with God-consciousness. Men are sincere when they sing to God.

The best of all songs are hymns; directed Godward, the upward reach of the soul draws forth the finest melodies. If you would be your best, sing to God.

All Christians are singing people. One of God's gifts to redeemed men is a new song; and one means by which He keeps them His own is the singing heart, in practice for the song of eternity. Conversely, all characteristically singing people are Christians; only Christians can sing "in the sunshine, in the shadow." Their song comes from a heart of joy; it stems from right relationship to the unchanging God.

"Open up to heaven all the windows of your soul," and let God tune your whole spirit to the harmonies of His home. Ask Him to give you a song in the morning and key all your day to its melody.

Keep a song in your heart; and as faith wafts it skyward,
The Saviour will listen, and heaven draw near.

—M. E. COVE

Lamp to My Feet

Acts 8:26-38

Search the scriptures; ... they ... testify of me (John 5:39).

How to Use the Bible for the Crisis. The Bible is usable. It was made for sinners; it is a saving agent for the crisis. It shows us God saving the world through Jesus. It shows us ourselves and our desperate need of salvation.

To understand the Bible is to see Jesus there. He is there from beginning to end: prophesied in Eden, foreshadowed in the books of the law, foretold by the prophets, incarnate in the Gospel story, exalted in the final Revelation. It is He who gives meaning and consistency to its 66 books. One verse here seems to contradict another there; but seen in relation to Christ, the jigsaw pieces all find their places and their meaning.

Jesus is the heart of Scripture; and the Cross is central in the gospel of Jesus. We cannot understand Jesus in relation to the types and prophecies nor to the consummation of His glory unless we see Him crucified as a sinless atonement for sinners. If He is merely an example, the pieces do not fit together.

To read the Bible with understanding is to see Jesus as dying for sinners to bring them to God. To believe with the heart is to go a step farther and see oneself as the one lost sinner whose name Jesus bears to the Father. It is to read His "whosoever" with one's name substituted; to hear His "Come unto me . . . and I will give you rest." When "wounded for *our* transgressions" has become "wounded for *my* transgressions," the Word has become personal and thus effective.

> *I will tell the wondrous story,*
> *How, my lost estate to save,*
> *In His boundless love and mercy*
> *He the ransom freely gave.*

Pray, and Faint Not

Matt. 6:9-13

He said unto them, When ye pray, say, Our Father . . . (Luke 11:2).

We *must pray*—probably the most important of all Bible directions for living the Christian life, and the most difficult. Jesus prayed—probably the strongest argument for our need of prayer.

Inspired directly by His perfect prayer habits and prayer technique, the disciples requested a lesson on prayer, and He responded immediately. He prayed himself, and He expects us to pray. He prayed effectively and acceptably to God; He expects His followers to learn to do the same.

How pray? Person to Person, directly. As a man to God, reverently, but as a child to Father, simply, trustfully; for we have been adopted into the family of heaven. Sincerely, in secret, with no eye to show or parade; for however many may be listening, we are closeted in spirit, shut in alone with God.

How pray? In orderly fashion. We are not to rush in to that Presence uttering the first words that come into our minds, or that come to our lips without ever reaching our minds. Of course, we are free to do so if we wish, but we may waste our words. God will pay attention when we pay attention.

Jesus suggests an order that takes time to realize first to whom we are speaking—first and last. If we would follow that suggestion faithfully, our prayers would have a grip of faith and power. Time can be wasted in saying prayers, but not in talking with God.

> *There's a blessing in prayer, in believing prayer,*
> *When our Saviour's name to the throne we bear.*
> *Then a Father's love will receive us there;*
> *There is always a blessing, a blessing in prayer.*

How Much Are You Worth?

John 1:19-31

I am the voice of one crying in the wilderness, Make straight the way of the Lord (John 1:23).

What do you think of yourself? A man's real worth can be measured from three points of view: his own, other people's, and God's. It will do us good to make a comparison of the three estimates. Are we rating ourselves too high or too low? Are we setting too high a value on popular opinion? How much does God's judgment weigh with us? Here is a good man, John.

John says he is a voice; he has forgotten himself in his message—that is all that counts. Livingstone had the same estimate of his own importance when he said, "I will place no value on anything I have or may possess except in its relation to the kingdom of Christ."

There is no virtue in self-abnegation or self-effacement, of itself. Everyone is a unique personality with a unique contribution to make to his day before he passes on. To forget oneself can be absentmindedness. John forgot himself in praising Jesus and preparing His way. His one contribution was as a forerunner; he counted himself of worth only as a herald of Jesus.

97

John knew that his message was unpopular, but he did not play up his suffering nor act the martyr; he did not bid for sympathy nor soft-pedal the message to save his skin. He did not consider himself important enough to worry much over. "Humility is not thinking oneself little, but thinking little of oneself."

Ready to speak, ready to think,
Ready with heart and brain,
Ready to stand where He sees fit,
Ready to bear the strain.

Remembering Him

Mark 14:22-25

This do in remembrance of me (Luke 22:19).

In Remembrance. That first Upper Room experience was the forerunner and prototype of many, many such experiences since. Life's "upper rooms" are the Christian's places of meeting with Jesus intimately, face-to-face and heart-to-heart. Jesus still is saying, "I must eat with My disciples."

One central direction for the sacrament cannot be legislated: "Remember." Remembering as Jesus meant it is a matter of heart understanding and appreciation. We cannot remember if we have never known.

The Last Supper was itself a commemoration. They were eating in memory of the Passover. Unless we know Jesus himself as the Paschal Lamb dying in our place, making everlasting atonement for our sins, we cannot eat "in remembrance of me." Sin bars the way.

In Anticipation. At the marriage supper of the Lamb we shall be with our Savior in fellowship, to go no more out

98

forever. Heaven is not primarily a place of relief from earthly trials and the happiness of indulged desires; heaven is a place of communion with Jesus. The Communion service gives us the opportunity to see how ready we are to enjoy that fellowship.

Remembering that Last Supper as Jesus meant it, we look forward as well as back. His farewell was linked with a promise; He said good-bye until the next meeting: *au revoir; auf Wiedersehen;* "till we meet again." I will take assurance; He wishes to see me again.

> *And when Thou sittest on Thy throne,*
> *Dear Lord, remember me.*

What a Savior!

Matt. 27:33-50

He is despised and rejected of men; a man of sorrows, and acquainted with grief (Isa. 53:3).

"Man of Sorrows." In mockery they labeled Him "King of the Jews," and His helplessness was an admission of their right to mock Him. Poor King this—He could not even protect himself!

Rejected by man, but more—rejected by God! The depth of that awful darkness was in the soul of Christ—separation from the Father. Identified with sin, He could not have God's smile. Sin is utter loneliness and isolation. It was agony for Him; it will be agony for all lost sinners who come to experience it.

Sin is not a harmless plaything. Sin is deadly poison. Sin is loathsome filth. But the sinless Christ must touch it, know it, be weighted down by it. "He . . . who knew no sin" became "sin for us." Only so could He tear us loose from it. Only so could a holy God root out the curse and restore the moral balance in the world.

"Darkness over the Land." The saddest, darkest hours the world has ever seen were the hours from twelve to three of the Crucifixion day. Life itself was gone with its Lord; the Sun of Righteousness was eclipsed in death. God had taken His protecting hand off His Son and, so it seemed, off His creation. It was the low point of all history, the crisis of the universe.

Jesus was spared nothing. He died outside the gate, of a piece with criminals and refuse. It was Satan's one short hour of empty triumph.

> *Well might the sun in darkness hide,*
> *And shut his glories in*
> *When Christ, the mighty Maker, died*
> *For man, the creature's, sin.*

"Risen, as He Said"

Luke 24:13-16, 28-43

But go your way, tell his disciples and Peter that he goeth before you into Galilee: there shall ye see him, as he said unto you (Mark 16:7).

Faithful. "What a Friend we have in Jesus." "Tell My disciples, especially Peter." Jesus has His eye on every one who has ever belonged to Him. He knows just where you are physically and spiritually. A failure should not make you hold back, but rather drive you to trust His yearning love. It is the enemy who tells you He does not care.

"He goeth before you." His, the thinking and planning; mine, the following. "All the way my Saviour leads me." Blessed new life of surprises fresh from the hand of my Lord! I cannot see the turns of the road ahead; but I know I shall find Him at every one.

"Ye shall see him." I do not have to go always by blind faith and dead reckoning. He has His own way of revealing himself to my heart, so real that I could doubt my own existence sooner than His. At every crisis He has not only sent an angel; he has been there himself. With that Presence nothing else matters.

"As he said." He keeps His promises. And He expects us to put each one of them to the test. I can stand stupidly wondering, or I can take Him at His word. Every promise is a challenge to action.

> *My chains fell off; my heart was free.*
> *I rose, went forth, and followed Thee.*

> *Who would not follow if he heard Him call?*

Rights and Responsibilities

Mic. 6:1-8

He hath shewed thee, O man, what is good (Mic. 6:8).

"*What doth the Lord require of thee, but . . . ?*" It sounds simple; it would recommend itself as a neat way of sloughing off creeds and vigorous demands and getting to the heart of an easy salvation. It is simple in that it highlights the essentials; it is not easy or relaxed. The agnostic Huxley was mistaken when he took it as his favorite text for a moralist's life. Rightly read, it demands what is impossible apart from Christ's salvation.

All life's myriad demands can be met by a right adjustment in three fields: ourselves, our neighbor, our God. We recognize our just responsibility in each relationship, and God adjusts our natures to enable us to fulfill it. So responsibility becomes privilege, and right living becomes natural.

"Do justly." That means that you settle once for all that God's will is your choice—nothing more, nothing less. You are neither leaner and parasite nor grasper and thief. With the spirit of contentment and the independence of adequate resources, you will not encroach on the rights of others. But this takes divine grace.

"Love mercy." You will not be satisfied with "Live and let live" as a motto. You recognize the debt that your strength owes to your brother's weakness. You will be a radiating center of kindness and forgiveness and helpfulness. This takes divine love.

"Walk humbly with thy God." This is the key that Huxley overlooked. The first of all the Beatitudes is for "the poor in spirit"; humility is the doorway to all Christian grace. Renouncing dependence on your own goodness, you commit yourself to complete dependence on God. So we found God; so we shall please God.

> *In a world wrapped in night*
> *Keep me pure, keep me white.*

102

His Handiwork

Ps. 104:1-24

O Lord, how manifold are thy works! in wisdom hast thou made them all (Ps. 104:24).

God of Mystery and Beauty. You can tell much about a person from his handiwork. So God must love beauty, variety, color, line, perspective, lights and shadows, proportion, symmetry. If He loves these in nature, He loves them in us. Think what that means. And be patient as He develops each in you.

God is the supreme Artist. As in nature, so in our lives, if we let Him turn His hand upon us. Cosmos (ordered beauty) out of chaos always in His work.

> *Dear Lord, take up the tangled strands*
> *Where we have wrought in vain,*
> *That by the skill of Thy dear hands*
> *Some beauty may remain.*

Or better, new beauty be created. It is His way.

God has poured out in nature a lavish profusion of beauty in sunrise and sunset, the fresh green of fields and the hazy blue of distant mountains, the riot of scarlet and gold and purple and rose in the common wildflowers. It was put there for a purpose: to lift us above the petty, often ugly, trivialities of life. And to remind us of "the beauty of holiness."

Where we see God, He is beautiful; where we do not see, He is still beautiful. This is not blind faith; it is the logic of sound reason.

103

God does not answer all our tortured questions about life. He covers himself and His deepest purposes. But He covers himself "with light." His answer to Job was His veiled manifestation of himself in the processes of nature.

> *Fair are the meadows; fairer still the woodlands,*
> *Robed in the blooming garb of spring.*
> *Jesus is fairer, Jesus is purer,*
> *Who makes the woeful heart to sing!*

"Expedient That I Go Away"

Acts 2:14-21, 32-33; Joel 2:28-29

And on my servants and on my handmaidens I will pour out in those days of my Spirit (Acts 2:18).

Pentecost: Personal; Positive. Pentecost marked the inauguration of a dispensation; but it was more. We cannot relegate it to past history any more than we can relegate Calvary. And God builds His kingdom with individuals. Individuals are brought nigh by the blood of the Cross; individuals receive the purging, Christ-revealing gift of the Spirit. There is no mass-empowering for service.

The Old and New Testaments both make plain that this blessing is for laity as well as for clergy, for young as well as for old, for women as well as for men. All become ministers of divine grace. It will take us all to save the world of sinners; and only witnesses can do the job.

God's plan is a beautiful, satisfying one. No one has to play second fiddle and take another person's word when it comes to testimony. No one has to depend on hearsay or shrink from giving his witness because someone else may know more about the case. An inner, direct word comes to everyone, and a compelling urge to tell it, as you want to tell any good news or recommend any wonderful cure. This grace is adapted to the normal way of normal people.

Nothing less will make an impression on the self-absorbed people we mingle with. To be Spirit-filled is to exert a positive influence. So long as you have Him, the inner pressure outward is stronger than the pressures from without that would make you cave in.

> Breathe on us now the Holy Ghost;
> Let each receive his Pentecost;
> Set hearts and tongues afire.

The Great Invitation

Isa. 55:4-13

They that seek the Lord shall not want any good thing (Ps. 34:10).

God promises satisfaction. God promises bread—that is, real food. Get salvation and your personality begins to build up in every way. Before that, though you were eating greedily, feverishly, you were always hungry. You were feeding on chaff. God's food makes you grow; your old diet was starving you.

God promises good. Good without qualification. Every human satisfaction has its fly in the ointment; God promises to work all things into good.

God, and God alone, promises life. It is undeniable that there are refined pleasures: music, reading, beauty in nature, in art, in human conduct. But all these are superficial and temporary unless illuminated by an adequate philosophy of life. Life must have its spiritual overtones to be complete.

God promises eternity. This should be the deciding factor. According to the great mathematician Pascal, even if there should prove to be no God and no endless life, people are insane not to choose God. For they must choose either for or against Him; and in this wager if they choose God they have everything to gain and nothing to lose. But if they choose against Him they stand to lose everything and gain nothing.

God promises usefulness. He called Israel both to blessing and to service. She was to be His proxy to the nations. She was to be an unswerving witness to idolatrous peoples of the glory of a holy God. There is no deeper satisfaction than to find oneself a vital part of a triumphing cause—God's.

> *Ho, ev'ry one that is thirsty in spirit!*
> *Ho, ev'ry one that is weary and sad!*
> *Come to the fountain; there's fullness in Jesus,*
> *All that you're longing for. Come and be glad.*

Everyday Praises

Psalm 122

I was glad when they said unto me, Let us go into the house of the Lord (Ps. 122:1).

"*I was glad.*" God, the Center of Everyday Living—this could well be the caption of the group of psalms we call the Pilgrim Psalter (120—134). Sung by the family units on the way to and from the Jerusalem feasts, these little poems are full of God and full of human experience. All talk about God is theory—perhaps insincere cant—until it is brought down to where we live. God becomes real to us only as He is al-

106

lowed to work on our human stuff, just as it is, in our human environment, just as we find it.

Real religion cannot be compartmentalized or shoved off into one area of living. It is in everything, or it is in nothing. It permeates every activity—of the man who has it.

And it permeates vitally, enthusiastically, dynamically, joyfully. If your religion is pale, colorless, lukewarm, you have been cheated into taking a substitute. A genuine faith in God is your healthy heart, pumping life into every part of you.

"The house of the Lord"; "I was glad"; "Let us go." Each of these phrases should have come alive to you if you are a purposeful Christian. God's revealed will is the spring and the goal of your activity, the spirit of gladness your mood, cooperation with other Christians your method—it is a good formula for well-adjusted living.

In one sense our relationship with God is an individual, personal matter; we go to heaven alone. In another sense it is a shared thing. Individual experiences shared give rise to the only pure fellowship known on earth; and in turn the sharing increases the personal blessing. We help ourselves to heaven as we help one another.

Come, we that love the Lord,
And let our joys be known.
. . . .
We're marching through Immanuel's ground,
To fairer worlds on high.

Practical Religion

James 2:14-26

For as the body without the spirit is dead, so faith without works is dead also (James 2:26).

James the Steady. How reassuring, and how right, that all varieties of temperaments and abilities find a welcome in the work of God! James is no lightning flash like Peter. He is slow in making up his mind; but once decided, he does not waver. He will never win as many converts as Peter or Paul; but he will help to "stablish, strengthen, settle" many who otherwise would fall away. God needs both types of servants.

"God grant me the serenity to accept things I cannot change, courage to change things I can, and wisdom to know the difference"—R. Niebuhr. Here is the peculiar genius of James: the ability to distinguish essentials from nonessentials and the character to act accordingly. Good sense for us all.

James the Practical. The author of The General Epistle of James is a practical Christian; and he gives us some of the secrets of a faith that permeates the deeps of the spirit and spreads into all of the contacts of life. He has lived, he has observed, he has studied himself and other people, and he gives us the benefit of his advice. It is worth more than money.

He starts with the practical man's view of life, which is his own: "Life's fine, powerful fine, but 'tain't easy." Settle it to go through, he says, and then cooperate with God. Grace doesn't provide an escape from life but a conquest of life.

The everyday treatment of your neighbor, the everyday use of your tongue, your money, and your prayer power—

these are the things that matter. If Christian, live as Christians, James says. He did so himself.

> In work that keeps faith sweet and strong,
> In trust that triumphs over wrong.

Jesus Began

John 17:6-21; Acts 1:1

I pray for them . . . that the world may believe that thou hast sent me (John 17:9, 21).

"Jesus began"; it echoes through the centuries. "Jesus began"—who finishes? Each generation holds Christ's trust afresh; it can implement or frustrate the grace of God. May it not be mine that fails Him!

Christ is seeking to save all men of all classes everywhere. And every individual has a thousand facets and a thousand avenues of approach. No two snowflakes are alike —much less two personalities. To win the world of men through men, Christ can use all types of workers and as many as He can get. Even our peculiar oddity can be the one means of approach to some soul. Put it into the Master's hands.

How desperately hemmed in you would be if you could not communicate with other persons by speech or even by hand movements, or if you could not move from place to place to execute your wishes! Christ is equally limited in His work on earth. His Holy Spirit speaks and acts through human personalities; He needs human tongues and eyes and hands and feet.

A foreigner is at the mercy of his interpreter; a government can be betrayed by its ambassador. So Christ has put himself at the mercy of His human representatives. We hold His interests in our hands. He is dependent on the interpretation we give Him today.

> *Let the beauty of Jesus be seen in me . . .*
> *O Thou Spirit divine,*
> *All my nature refine,*
> *Till the beauty of Jesus be seen in me.*

God's Great Man

Ps. 18:46-50

The Lord is my rock, and my fortress, and my deliverer; my God, my strength, in whom I will trust (Ps. 18:2).

Humanity Made Great. David was a many-sided personality. He distinguished himself as great warrior, great ruler, great poet, and great musician. But it is as a man that we know him best; in fact, we know him as we know few men of history. Here too he is "great": magnanimous, high-visioned, intense; deeply and broadly human. In him we see mirrored our own joys and sorrows, our sins and our salvation. He speaks for us all as we could not speak for ourselves. We are glad that David lived.

David had some very human failings, and one heartbreaking plunge into an orgy of sin. We cannot call him ideal. Yet God pronounced him a man after His own heart. David, like us, must claim God's grace for forgiveness and cleansing and have sins removed "as far as the east is from the west." He said so. Our hearts are one with his.

The real secret of David's greatness is that he filled his life with God. There have been other many-faceted personalities of vast gifts who shriveled with selfishness or hardened with pride. David shows us how rich and strong and full humanity can be if it opens itself to Deity. Man was made for God; David helps us realize how truly.

You too can stretch your soul or shrink it; the difference lies in whether you fill it with God or merely with yourself. You may not be much to start with; but if you turn over every faculty and every interest to God, He will enrich·them in a way that will surprise you.

> *Frail children of dust, and feeble as frail,*
> *In Thee do we trust, nor find Thee to fail.*
> *Thy mercies how tender! how firm to the end!*
> *Our Maker, Defender, Redeemer, and Friend!*

The Road to Freedom

Exod. 15:1-18

The Lord is my strength and song, and he is become my salvation (Exod. 15:2).

Emancipated. What is your special bondage? Who is your Pharaoh? Fear? habit? moods? circumstances? Not one can hold you a moment longer if you will claim your freedom. The Emancipation Proclamation has been signed. Or hadn't you heard? Let the great Emancipator handle your chains.

Triumphantly delivered is well begun. The assurance of initial salvation is a guaranty for the future. That first radio message of peace that swept into your heart assured you that you need never fear again, for God was equal to all your need. A sound conversion tells us what we can depend on for the rest of our lives. Those who have guessed about their conversion will be guessing about all the rest.

Some principles are established at the outset: (1) God will take care of our enemies; all we need is to follow directions. (2) Guidance will be given as we need it; the pillar of cloud will always go before. (3) The only safety is staying on God's side; the cloud is blackness for His enemies. Here is a sufficient recipe for conditional security.

Deliverance such as this, experienced by the individuals making up the Church of God, remembered and repeated; principles such as these, trusted and explored—then we might pray without mockery, "Thy will be done in earth, as it is in heaven." This is our sad old world's only hope. Could we try it yet today? At least we could make a start.

> Then forward still, 'tis Jehovah's will,
>   Though the billows dash and spray.
> With a conqu'ring tread we will push ahead;
>   He'll roll the sea away.

"Give Ye Them to Eat"

Mark 6:33-34, 53-56

[He] was moved with compassion toward them, because they were as sheep not having a shepherd (Mark 6:34).

"*He was moved with compassion.*" To enjoy Christ's gift of fellowship with himself we must share His *compassion.* Complacency parts company with Christ—most of all, the spiritual complacency that sings, "I'm satisfied," with no outreach of heart to those who are hungry and lost.

Compassion says that nothing else matters in comparison with the needs of lost men. Rest and food and the business of living all can be postponed when souls are at stake. Interruptions of legitimate plans at compassion's call

112

are not detours. If Jesus had not interrupted His vacation, we never should have had the miracle of the 5,000 fed.

"He went about the villages." We must share His *aggressiveness.* Jesus offered His grace to men who were indifferent; He came to those who did not ask for Him. He did not wait to be invited; He made the first move. His approach first alerted them to their deepest need. We too cannot expect sinners to seek us out; we must go where they are; we must find ways to make them realize their lostness and Christ's love; we must not run away at the first rebuff.

Jesus sent His disciples out. He could have dispatched an angel to earth or drawn men by some mysterious influence. He did neither. Person must touch person in this world of personality values.

> *Seeking the lost, yes, kindly entreating*
> *Wanderers on the mountain astray;*
> *"Come unto Me," His message repeating,*
> *Words of the Master speaking today.*

The Stewardship of Money

Ps. 50:7-15; Deut. 8:6-14

When thou hast eaten and art full . . . beware that thou forget not the Lord (Deut. 8:10-11).

Stewardship. Money is not a dead thing; it is very much alive. It represents what you have given your life for: your abilities, your time, your physical and mental energy. You can no more be careless of it than of any other of your talents.

We must see money for what it is if we are to give it its right place in our lives. A proper regard for money will make us spend it wisely; a clinging love for money will ruin us.

113

Money is as powerful and as dangerous as dynamite. Wisely invested, it can save souls; misused, it can destroy and damn.

Money is almost omnipotent; it can move mountains. So money is deceitful. You can begin to feel that it can buy you anything you want. You begin to clutch it and scramble for it. You begin to love it for itself. Then you are its slave; it has you.

"To him that knoweth to do good, and doeth it not, to him it is sin." How about us, I wonder, when we have heard statistics piled up repeatedly? Stewards are required to weigh values and make wise decisions, then act.

The principle of stewardship is clearly enunciated in the Old Testament. It runs like this: (1) Everything belongs to God. (2) He has lent each of us some material things, as well as the ability to increase our store. (3) He expects us to acknowledge His ownership by returning a share of the profits. (4) If we are faithful in our obligation, we shall prosper. The lawgiver and the Psalmist and the wise man were confident that the principle worked.

Far better than gold or wealth untold
Are the riches of love in Christ Jesus.

Forget Not

Ps. 103:13-22

The Lord is good to all: and his tender mercies are over all his works (Ps. 145:9).

"Who redeemeth thy life." Thank Him for His utter faithfulness. People said it would ruin you if you took His way. But how marvelously He has kept His word at every turn! How He has made and kept appointments! How He has

opened doors to service and filled the gaps of your insufficiency! How through the days and years He has done the exceeding abundant! Look back, and praise.

Thank Him for undertaking to fight your battles and to take care of your reputation. Thank Him that truth is certain to come out on top in the end. How this confidence frees you from worry and anxiety! Just one concern, then: to be true to God and truth. He will care for the rest.

Count in the opportunities of blessing and usefulness He gives you. Your life is so far removed from destruction that it is made a positive, creative force in His universe. Thank Him for the prayers He allows you to pray and the good words He puts in your heart to say this day. There is no wretchedness much worse than to feel oneself useless and unemployed. His children are never derelicts.

Don't take God for granted. He can safely double up His blessings on a grateful person.

Thank Him for making Deity available to humanity. Say to Him, as you have sometimes said to a friend after trying your best to express thanks for a gift: "Thank You for yourself —better than all gifts." Thank God for being who He is, and our Friend.

> *For as high as is the heaven . . .*
> *Is the tender mercy He doth ever show.*

"Greater Is He That Is in You"

1 Cor. 3:11-17; 9:24-27

For ye are bought with a price: therefore glorify God in your body, and in your spirit, which are God's (1 Cor. 6:20).

Christian Convictions. Two rules the Bible gives us for dealing with . . . non-Christian pressures; in some way both must be followed. The first is Christian convictions; the second, Christian love. One has to do with our relations to God and self; the other concerns our relations to God and people. The first has to do with personal integrity; the second, with personal influence.

The rule of Christian convictions is more than "not doing." It is not doing *because* . . . It is the independence of spirit to recognize oneself as living under the laws of another world, the servant of God while the world looks on.

Where do we get the content of our convictions? Christian ideals first—Bible principles, the Word of God interpreted according to our best understanding. Then Christian precedents—the customs, practices, standards of the most spiritual Christians through the centuries. We do not have to guess. The things the Bible frowns on, the things Christians have found hindrances to Christian living—I want none of these. I need not start fresh, experimenting.

I cannot always find specific practices mentioned in Scripture; I can find the principle to include every practice. More than that, I can find the all-embracing loyalty to include every principle. The all-inclusive pressures are two, appetite and custom: "I'd like to do it," "Everybody's doing it." The all-inclusive Christian principle is loyalty to the will of God: my body and mind at their best for God, my influence at its best for God.

> *Each vict'ry will help you*
> *Some other to win.*
>
> . . . .
>
> *Look ever to Jesus;*
> *He'll carry you through.*

116

The Grade A Christian

Acts 26:12-19

Lord, what wilt thou have me to do? (Acts 9:6).

A Great Christian. What makes a great Christian? I should like to know. It is my chosen vocation, and there is a place for holy ambition. I believe they say that the apostle Paul reached the top; I will listen to what he has to say as he weighs his own experience.

A Christian experience is great in proportion to its reality. A vast deal that passes for Christianity is cant; that is, words we use without ever testing their meaning. It is much simpler to talk about good things than to live them. The proof of sincerity, Paul says, is in the difficult places of down-to-earth living. "We have only so much religion as we have in the emergency," which is too much for our natural goodness.

Bunyan wrote of Mr. By-Ends, who came from the town of Fair-Speech, that he was all for Religion when she went in her silver slippers. And I knew a girl whose mother told her she was a wonderful Christian when everything went her way. The power of Christ is put on display in us when things do not go our way. And we show our loyalty to Religion most effectively when she must go in rags and we still stand by her.

A Christian is not great—though he may be prominent thereby—because he has money or background or personality; not because he has firm convictions or orthodox beliefs or even mystical revelations and ecstatic experiences. He is a great Christian to the extent of his undramatic, practical acquiescence in the will of God.

> *Take my will and make it Thine;*
> *It shall be no longer mine.*

117

Jesus, My King

Col. 1:9-19

That in all things he might have the preeminence (Col. 1:18).

How can I honor Him as King today? I can obey Him, even at the cost of an upheaval in my ways and habits as complete as took place that terrifying day in the Temple. It may mean just that—if my ways are not right in His sight. I can trust His truth.

I can praise Him with lips and with life. I can cultivate in my daily fellowship with Him that close personal relationship that makes Him fairest of 10,000 and altogether lovely; and I can do my best to let Him and others know that He is "Wonderful." I can cry, "Hosanna," not only one day, but every day.

I can serve as He served. I can choose the Cross as He chose it. I can align my life with His, not trying to pull His teaching down to the level of my selfish life. I can follow His way and receive honor from God, not men.

I can build my life into His kingdom by serving and giving and loving according to His standards and His example. He will show me how to be doing this even in what seem the trivial choices of this day.

I can hold my goods and my time at His disposal—and be grateful that He asks. For so He allows me a great investment.

I can be loyal to Him when everyone else seems against Him. Even when the name King is written over a cross, I can stand by. I shall not lose by utter trust in the King.

Jesus, my Lord, I'll ever adore Thee,
Lay at Thy feet my treasures of love.
Lead me in ways to show forth Thy glory,
Ways that will end in heaven above.

Wonderful Words of Life

Ps. 19:7-14

The law of thy mouth is better unto me than thousands of gold and silver (Ps. 119:72).

How to value the Bible. The longer we live, the more wonderful we see God's gift of the Holy Scriptures to be. As life becomes more tangled and complex and we see men and women falling by the wayside, mentally unbalanced or morally wrecked because they have tried to muddle through alone, we rejoice humbly in the assurance of an infallible, unchanging revelation.

The Bible is both "law" and "testimony," that is, the character and will of God revealed and the saving grace of Jesus Christ made known. We see here God's holiness and His demand that we be holy; and here, praise God, we learn of the Calvary redemption. The Bible gives us all knowledge necessary to salvation.

The Bible gives "statutes" and "commandments"; it tells us what is eternally right. Second only to the revelation of salvation from sin by Jesus Christ is the gift of the moral law. Here is lifted for us the immutable standard of righteousness; here are defined the everlasting principles governing the relationship of man to God and of man to man. To live by these is harmony and happiness. To disregard these is to break yourself against them.

The Bible is full of God. It exalts God as all-wise, all-powerful, all-good. This faith, this fear, is the one solid basis of enduring success and of upright character. It is safe to trust God's knowledge, God's standards, God's commissions always, and to build one's life upon them. The Bible furnishes this constant in an unstable world.

> *Sing them over again to me,*
> *Wonderful words of life!*
> *Let me more of their beauty see,*
> *Wonderful words of life!*

The Patience of Consecration

Luke 9:51-62

I am crucified with Christ: nevertheless I live; yet not I, but Christ liveth in me (Gal. 2:20).

No consecration is valid unless it is acted upon. Carry the cross.

There is something fascinating, almost romantic, about the idea of consecration. *Living* a consecration has in it the grind of monotony and the rack of suffering. You will be tried to your human limit and beyond. But consecration is meant for living, or it is nothing.

The cross is no one duty or trial. The cross is a lifelong attitude and relationship. You take it up once for all when you yield your will, and you never lay it down till life is over. It becomes a part of your self.

120

The mission of the Cross was the goal of Christ's life on earth. The call of the Cross determined His choices and directed His steps. The shadow of the Cross controlled His desires. The arms of the Cross exposed Him to shame and broke His heart. And for us the cross accepted means giving up personal wishes, ambitions, ease, reputation, even life itself at the will of God. Real consecrations are not made easily or lightly.

The hardest thing to die to is what we call our "rights." Jesus' cross should close our mouths to any claim of rights.

"I'll pay the price, whatever others do"—you sang it, with the thrill of others joining with you. You keep your word alone, with others unsympathetic or antagonistic. Consecration is between you and God.

> *The Cross! the Cross! that Blood-stained Cross!*
> *The hallowed Cross I see!*
> *Reminding me of precious Blood*
> *That once was shed for me.*

Learners of Jesus

Matt. 10:1, 5-15

Learn of me (Matt. 11:29).

Disciples learn. Children grow up. Followers go somewhere. Servants do something. These are the terms used to describe Christians. When we are born again we enter upon an active, progressing life. We are saved for a purpose. Watch what Jesus did with the Twelve in the few years He was with them. He wishes to do the same for us. He will be Teacher if we will be learners. It is our only way to grow.

Jesus' followers follow Him in spirit. So they learn to serve without becoming servile; for every menial act is done for the King. They become superior to cheap public sentiment, for they trust the eternal truth.

They learn that they must not sell out to people, nor bind people's devotion to themselves. Sooner or later—it should be sooner—every Christian must sign a declaration of independence, and a declaration of supreme loyalty. This fine freedom is impossible apart from grace; but it is essential to growth in grace.

They learn an eternal antagonism to the unclean and impure. They learn to take the offensive against sin and Satan. Your hatreds are as important as your loves; and there is a duty of hatred. Unless you hate evil supremely, you will let it override you or cajole you.

They learn the lesson of trust in a Heavenly Father. They learn to commit themselves recklessly to the divine provision, to shut the door on anxiety about how they will fare when obedience costs bread and butter and nice clothes. It is easier to worry or to scheme than to wait for God, but this lesson is part of the discipleship course. And the heavenly supply house is not bankrupt.

> *More like the Master I would ever be,*
> *More of His meekness, more humility;*
> *. . . more courage to be true.*

God's Stabilizing Program

Exod. 20:1-7; 28:9-12

*I am the Lord thy God. . . . Thou shalt have no other gods before
me* (Exod. 20:2-3).

Worship is central. "We stand or fall on worship." We need
to remember it. When God set out to build a nation after His
own heart, He made worship central. He put the Tabernacle
in the midst of the camp and related every soul to it.

The names of all the tribes were inscribed on the priest's
ephod. So our names are written on our Savior's wounded
hands and carried by Him into the Father's presence. This
personal relationship with himself God counts important. Yet
there are those who boast of a religion of good works or of
self-mastery. God puts himself at the heart of true religion.

The demand that worship be primary is not arbitrary or
unkind, nor is the "jealousy" of Jehovah petty. He knows it is
for our good in this world as well as in the next to set our
hearts on Him. If we have twined our affections and our
hopes around any human being or any earthly thing, when
we lose that we are adrift, unbalanced, uprooted. God knows
that He is the one changeless Center for any life.

A right relationship with God is the stabilizer for life. It
is the guaranty of permanence and right perspective, and of
sound personal and public relations. When I look often into
the face of God to realize my dependence on Him and be
guided by His eye, I am not likely to pick a fuss with my
hot-tempered neighbor or tear my life to pieces with unholy

123

appetites. I have a principle of control. All praise for this inner constant.

> *O Thou who changest not,*
> *Abide with me.*

The Balanced Life

John 2:1-11

Whatsoever he saith unto you, do it (John 2:5).

Just Everyday with a Plus. In Jesus the Man was perfect balance; our first view of Him in action shows us all of life with the balance perfect between "secular" and "religious." Jesus as man lived a normal life, with its work and its worship and its play; but in all of this He never loses that Jesus-as-God authority. His life is our example, and His words are our guide.

There is an "everyday" side to life, but it need not be secularized—it must not be. Jesus at the wedding feast shows us how a complete Christian lives every day: He is friendly, interested in people and their interests, approachable, helpful. He is not ingrown; all His assets are at the disposal of others.

Jesus at the wedding feast shows us what God can do for us practically in the ordinary demands and the unexpected emergencies of life (every day brings them). He supplies what we lack—our best always comes short; He will perform miracles if necessary, just to make life run smoothly. But He can help us only if in every detail we are unquestioningly obedient.

The common run of living loses its sameness when we take it from Christ's hands. He will turn life's water to wine.

Every prosaic task done at His command and under His direction has its own exhilarating thrill; and His thrills have the best taste.

> *There's within my heart a melody.*
> *Jesus whispers sweet and low:*
> *"Fear not, I am with thee; peace, be still,"*
> *In all of life's ebb and flow.*

Trial of Your Faith

1 Pet. 1:1-9

Think it not strange concerning the fiery trial which is to try you, as though some strange thing happened unto you (1 Pet. 4:12).

Temptation. Better develop a wholesome respect for temptation. Peter and the others said confidently, "We are able." Jesus rebuked their superficial self-assurance. Only if your spirit has been prepared, He said, dare you risk meeting the inevitable tests ahead.

Count on trials: the "fire." Think of temptation as God's refining process; it is. Not yet in heaven, you are still on probation. Think of your temptations as necessary. Satan does not mean them so; he sends them to ruin you. But God utilizes them for His purposes. He is tempering you for heaven and for service. Remember Job's word, "He knoweth . . . when he hath tried me, I shall come forth as gold." When you emerge, you will be worth more to God and to others.

Expect temptations that are "fiery": sheer torture, humanly unendurable. Any temptation that really is temptation is either so overwhelming in its intensity or so confusing in its subtlety that it is a new thing, too difficult or too surprising for us to cope with. Nobody, it seems, ever faced just this;

prepare as we might, we never looked for this. We must have divine grace to carry us through.

Then remember Christ. Accept your temptations as one aspect of your fellowship with Christ; inescapable for His followers, endurable by His presence and His help, rewardable at His coming. He did not ask exemption; nor will we.

> *When through fiery trials thy pathway shall lie,*
> *My grace, all-sufficient, shall be thy supply.*
> *The flame shall not hurt thee; I only design*
> *Thy dross to consume and thy gold to refine.*

There Is an End

Mark 13:1-8, 24-32; 2 Pet. 3:8-14

Heaven and earth shall pass away: but my words shall not pass away (Mark 13:31).

Count on the Certainties of the Future. Change is certain. The world as we know it is only an hour in God's long day and is scheduled to pass as one hour glides into the next. How shall we feel when our familiar world has gone, and only we and God remain?

The date when the present scheme of things shall finally be dissolved is unknown. But it is foolish to pretend that the world we know is not in process of dissolution. Some institutions that seemed to us as stable as the solid rock have gone overnight. The upheavals of our decade are preparing us for the end.

God's Word is certain. The destruction of the supposedly everlasting Temple came as Christ had said. Step by step the prophecies have been fulfilled; we have only to watch the climax come to pass. It is as sure as God is sure.

The return of Christ to claim His faithful saints is certain. The "signs of the times" to them are whispers of His near arrival and of their promotion. Is it not worth close fellowship with Him daily to maintain this understanding? That is what it costs.

The safety of Christ's "elect" is certain. He is coming to claim them. He is watching that the suffering shall not be too fierce nor too prolonged. The elect are those who have identified themselves with Him; they chose to be His chosen.

The thought of the Judgment is sobering but not frightening for Christians. They are to think of it often; they are to live every day in the light of that final day. They are to make it, not a doomsday, but a payday.

> *Ready in life, ready in death,*
> *Ready for His return.*

God's Eternal Now

Deuteronomy 30

He is thy life, and the length of thy days (Deut. 30:20).

We have, best of all, God. God confronts us today with a new covenant for ratification. But He will not have us sign until we have taken a long look in three directions. This is to be a great divide: one of those days that determine all the days that shall come after—the day at God's altar when we consecrate ourselves forever.

Look back, He says, at the past. Remember the Red Sea with the God who delivers from sin's bondage, and the wilderness journeying with the God who protects from enemies and supplies all needs. When we choose to obey God without reserve we are not taking a leap in the dark; we are trusting ourselves to a Person we know. And what a Person!

Look ahead, He says, to the future. There is My purpose for you: safety, plenty, never-stale satisfaction, with Me as your Refuge, your Security, your Victory. There too is My warning: no happiness apart from Me. Should you forget Me, blessing will turn to curse.

Look beyond, He says, and look up. For there is enabling power. In Joshua's day the promise was dim, but to us it is clear, in Jesus and His salvation. We are living in an outworn dispensation if we grind on by duty only; there is the compulsion of love in the look at Jesus.

God confronts us today with a new commandment—old as God is old, but freshly imperative upon us, as if we never heard it before. He enunciates it plainly and presses it home. He shows it as a life-and-death matter. It is this: Love enough to obey, or be lost.

> *O Rock divine, O Refuge dear . . .*
> *Be Thou our Helper ever near,*
> *A Shelter in the time of storm.*

The Old, New Story

John 1:9-18; 1 John 4:7-10

The fruit of the Spirit is love, joy, peace (Gal. 5:22).

Implications of the Christmas story. Christ's coming brought the fruit of the Spirit within our reach. The Fall had introduced chaos into human nature; a new cosmos must be let down from above to resolve its discords. It came with Christ; our answer still is in Him.

128

The love of God revealed in Christ gave us the everlasting pattern for character and conduct. The love of God imparted through faith in Christ gives us the power for harmonious living and the secret of genuine poise.

Through Jesus peace comes to individuals, and so to the world. But this is a peace that "passeth understanding"; it too comes down from above, wherever restless men and women hand over to Christ their unmanageable problems—sins, cares, distresses—and find instead trust, thanksgiving, and a steady calm. The fighting spirit has gone.

Jesus' coming is joy in essence: the open door from curse to blessing, from slavery to freedom, from darkness to light. For it tells us we can live in the Spirit; we can escape from the bondage of corruption to the glorious liberty of the sons of God. If only our hearts sing, the weight of the years is lifted.

The implications of Christmas are summed up in a transformed spirit through faith in Jesus; a new way of living follows. It is His Spirit working out: "longsuffering, gentleness, goodness, faith, meekness, temperance [self-control]." I want to celebrate this Christmas by accepting His gift to me of the Holy Spirit, whom He sent to make His presence a lasting reality.

> *Joy to the world! the Saviour reigns;*
> *Let men their songs employ.*

5

Autobiographical

From the Preface

They tell me I must write my autobiography. High-sounding term for such an uneventful story as mine. A long life, as counted in years, spent almost entirely in one spot on one job—what is there to tell? Yet to me every day has been exciting and new; "boredom" is a word I do not know. And my heart has traveled to the ends of the earth with the students I have loved. Perhaps I should try to put some of it in words.

How tell it from the perspective of the '80s? How see it? Perhaps Emerson will say it best for me: "The years teach what the days did not know."

A Life Perspective

In a sense always a pioneer, traveling an untried path, I can see spot after spot where one false step could have plunged me into an abyss; crossroads where the wrong road would have been easier to take than the right; a single Yes instead of a No, or vice versa, a single thought could have made the difference between heaven and hell. Some of these crucial spots I can identify, some record; many I am unaware of. The marvel that this frail self has come through, even after a fashion, amazes me, stirs me to the depths. I am glad John Newton wrote "Amazing Grace":

> Through many dangers, toils, and snares
> I have already come.
> 'Tis grace has brought me safe thus far,
> And grace will lead me home.

That "me" shows marks of batterings. But something in me sings in humble gratitude, "It is well, it is well with my soul." And has been well, far beyond any deserving of mine.

. . . The years have taught me more about this "soul." They have given me more than a fatalistic dependence on happenstance, or even a blind trust to a magic protection from harm in life's chances and changes. They have shown me that I am not a helpless pawn or a bouncing shuttlecock in a game between the forces of good and evil. I have something to say about what becomes of me. Every "self" is more than self-aware; it is self-directing. It has a will. The chances and changes are beyond our power, but the total picture is "chances and changes, and *choices*."

Heredity and environment are strong, but will is stronger, and when linked with God, invincible. Even our wills are not enough to carry us through, but a life committed fully to God is indestructible, undestroyable—safe.

Early Sense of Responsibility

That speech in the story of Joseph's brothers got hold of me: Judah's plea, "How shall I go up to my father, and the lad be not with me?" It haunted me for years; in fact, it has never left me. It connected itself with the tragedy of the rich young ruler; with our young men. I tried to put into verse what it said to me:

THE GARDEN OF THE LORD

A charge to keep,
The garden of the Lord to tend;
And then His words to hear at evening time,
Praise or rebuke.

One day, upon an old Judean road,
Strong, fine, and clean,
High-hearted, eager-eyed,

134

Mind like a keen, sure blade,
Youth met the Master.
And the Lord, beholding, loved him:
Loved him for dawning visions
Of service, purity, achievement rare,
Loved him, yet did not spare.
Called him to leave the low and choose the high,
To live not for his day but for eternity:
Showed him the life that finds its good in giving;
Challenged to strip himself of every weight and run the
    race,
Lost to earth's golden apples, following Christ alone.

Our charge to keep, these clear-eyed ones He loves;
The garden of the Lord to tend—
How shall we come at last before our Father,
The lad left behind?

I wrote this of my own sense of responsibility, but I believe I expressed the spirit of every faculty member [at ENC].

An Anniversary Inventory

(30th Anniversary Year—1949)

When I say ENC:

I see 500 clean, earnest young men and women who have chosen the genuine things and who really believe the will of God is life's highest good—believe it enough to act accordingly.

I see a group of faculty members to whom persons are worth more than things and a place of service worth more than money; who are here because God called them here.

135

I see alumni from Canada to California, from Washington to Florida, and all around the world: a college president here, a seminary dean and professors there; a superintendent of nurses here, a superintendent of schools there; a physician, a teacher, a missionary, an upright businessman; Christian homes and holiness churches; Christian fathers and mothers sending their children back to ENC from the ends of the earth.

I see a venture of faith that has proved it is always safe to obey and trust God. ENC is the impossible realized through the blessing of God. ENC is answered prayer—and so is a constant challenge to faith for the next impossibility.

I see a college which always has had for its goal the balance that the educators are beginning to cry for: the sound scholastic standards, the general cultural education, *plus* the "social conscience" and the Christian spirit. I hear the dean of a large graduate school say, "The students that come from that little college *have* something."

For I see a place that God has kept His hand upon and has brought to a day of unparalleled opportunity. I see potentialities that can bless the world and make ENC a praise in the earth.

ENC's brick buildings, we never forget, are born of that God-given vision, more than 30 years ago in the small corner room of the worn frame building in Rhode Island, ENC's forerunner, to three persons praying together; "a group of brick buildings—ours." Impossible. But today, through God and His people that vision is being realized.

God-given, too, is the larger vision of a holiness college in the East that shall stand until Jesus comes. The Christian college is vital to the work of God. In the years when young people are making their longtime choices—of vocation, companionship, philosophy of life—it makes it natural for them

136

to choose right. It urges them to know God for themselves and to make those choices through Him.

Our vision today:

An *atmosphere* where education will never choke out the love of God; where God is real in Christ; where His knowledge, His standards, His commissions are trusted implicitly.

Teachers who are investing in young people. Called of God, their lives interpret the truth they teach.

Sound preparation for life and Christian service: reputable scholastic standards and adequate equipment; a variety of training for ministry and laity.

A sterling product in young lives saved to the Kingdom and directed into the useful channels of God's choice. Holiness in action; education poised and aglow.

ENC a praise in the earth.

I O U

The following, published originally in the *Herald of Holiness,* I believe expresses my philosophy of personal relations:

I owe you respect for your personality. You too are that climax of God's creation, made in His likeness. I owe you a right to your own opinion. You may differ with me without fear that I shall raise a barrier between us if we do not see eye to eye. We can disagree and still be friends.

I owe you belief in your integrity. Since I do, I shall put the best possible construction on your actions. I shall trust your words and deeds, even those I am unable to understand.

I owe you honest treatment; I shall not steal people's good opinion of you. I shall voice the sort of comment on you and your actions that I should wish made on me.

I owe you a "taking-off place." Though I value your friendship, I shall not enslave your spirit nor bind you so closely to me that you will lose the wealth of other friendships, or even fail to develop your own best potentialities.

I owe you thoughtful consideration. I will not steal your time when you are evidently busy, just because I happen to have some free time to "kill."

I owe you honest wages if I chance to be employer, honest work if I chance to be employed, honest measure and just weight in any case.

I owe you special help in time of special need: my hand, my ear, my voice. I owe you patience with what seems to me your stupidity or slowness. I owe you the identification of Golden Rule imagination. I owe you "love unfeigned."

I owe it to you not to push you down in order to lift myself. Rather, I owe you advancement to the limit of my ability. I owe it to you to see you forge ahead of me without any reaction of envy or jealousy—even to give you a push.

I owe you a good example, a Christian testimony. I owe you the gospel of Christ to the limit that I possess it. I owe it to you to prove its power to the full, that God may challenge and encourage you by the sight of what He has done for someone else.

All this I owe you, and much more. I owe it to you not to fall behind with my payments. I shall always owe the abounding love that will meet those unforeseen and unexpected demands of the emergency and will save me from "Thou shalt" and "I must."

"Owe no man any thing, but to love."

My Philosophy of Education

I arrived at the following tentative formulation of a philosophy of Christian education. No doubt it has glaring philosophical weaknesses, but I am writing a personal record, not defending a thesis. . . .

My philosophy . . . starts with a basic commitment to essential revealed truth.

GOD: *Creator,* infinite in knowledge and goodness
Love to man shown in redemption
Personal: self-knowing, self-directing

MAN: *Created,* finite
Image of God: self-knowing
A whole being who thinks, feels, wills, acts
Potential: God-given sovereignty of his own
Ability to choose: Harmony with God
or
Opposition, alienation

Redemption and Revelation
Primary: God in Christ, God the Spirit
Secondary: In the Scriptures; in the Church of Christ
(Through these, redemption of individual men; through individual men, redemption of society)

Education: development of the potential

Christian Education: true and safe development of redeemed, regenerated, restored men
Note: Man naturally is out of harmony with God through a perverse will.

139

Traces of the divine image remain in a sensitivity of spirit and attraction to the drawing of the Holy Spirit.

The task, work, responsibility of the church is to regenerate (begin).

The task, work, responsibility of the college is to develop.

In evangelizing the student, the college is laying the foundation of a sound education. (She must often assume the role of the church.) The faculty member is not responsible to indoctrinate or to require the student to accept God's will or his own ideas; he is responsible to let him know and help him to understand how he himself has related himself to God, and his subject to the basic Christian philosophy.

Specifically, the work of Christian education is:

1. To accept, if necessary, or supplement the *role of the church* for the initial step: a yielded will, an opened heart.

2. To lead the student to *accept* the fact of Christ as the one authentic Revelation of God to man, to *commit* himself to that as a guiding principle, and to explore its implications.

3. With the student to *seek truth* from every source, truth to be apprehended through all faculties (intellect, imagination, emotions, will) and to be expressed in action. The understood goal: dynamic integration of "the life of the mind" and "the life of the spirit."

4. To *guide* the student in *finding* and *checking* discovered "truths" with the essentials of revealed truth (the teachings of Christ and His life, death, and resurrection).

5. To *think with* the student in exploring and discovering new facets of already apprehended truth, revealed or discovered; in relating, organizing, and assimilating all so gathered and tested truth, distinguishing primary, eternal, absolute

values from secondary, temporary values subject to question, change, or modification.

6. To aid the student through all possible means—example, communication, involvement, commitment, participation—to express in *action* the truth being made his.

7. And so, to aid in developing his God-given, Christ-redeemed, and Spirit-guided-and-energized personality for utmost service to God and men in this world and for an eternity of growth in knowledge of the Triune God and His purposes.

Church Membership and Responsibility

I have loved the church and tried to be a faithful member. Possibly too faithful; for I have probably missed some fine things in Boston churches, and certainly the delight of slipping in to hear some of our alumni pastors and see their congregations. But church membership to me involved responsibility. And my understanding of the Golden Rule has made me a front-seater. I know how a speaker feels facing empty seats. Also how much closer the fellowship when near the speaker and near one another.

My Weaknesses

Weaknesses? Many. And more show up with the years. "Old age is an accumulation of bad habits." In all honesty I must say that it is only the most bothersome, and obvious, to which I now confess.

Number One, that unique to me, dubious grade of B++, revealing indecision of character, but intended (am I rationalizing?) to suggest to the student that with a grain of determined effort he might earn the coveted A−−.

Number Two, my "files," which I fear reveal a shameless lack of system, but which I excuse by saying that I never had a full-time secretary. One part-time student secretary, Mary Sumner (Lechner), one of the extremely few *summa cum laude* graduates in ENC history, did her best to put my house in order, but her term of service was short. Mary Wallace and Doreen Armstrong (Pratt) also did what they could, but they too were shared with the registrar.

Number Three, which may be distantly related to the secretary problem, but which probably makes closer connection with the bad reputation of good intentions: the manila envelopes filled with open and read letters, discovered when necessity drives me to clear out desk drawers, labeled, "Answer at Once." . . .

But with the weaknesses, the promises grasped and the understanding love of a Christ who shared our humanity. I read today of "the two persuasions." "I know whom I have believed, and am persuaded that he is able to keep"—Christ's faithfulness. "I am persuaded that [nothing] . . . shall be able to separate us from the love of God, which is in Christ Jesus"—Christ's love. . . .

I recall President Mann's testimony that he had learned to live a normal Christian life by walking, using both feet: one foot Trust, the other Obey. Trust—Obey—Trust—Obey. It is a good march rhythm. . . .

Best of all is the fact that, in spite of all my dissatisfaction with myself, His Spirit has constantly been with me. John 13 and 17 has been to me the sine qua non. At the end of all I fling myself on His unutterable mercy, crying, "Blessed are they that hope in His mercy."

On Triumphant Living

As I come to the close of my chronicle, I recall that somewhere I have claimed to have had "not a moment of boredom" in my teaching. I trust I have not given a wrong impression. Boredom, no. Weariness of mind and body, frustration and perplexity, yes. Once asked if I enjoyed grading papers, I replied, "No, most of them." I stopped to think, "No, I don't like correcting papers. I really suffer over assigning grades—but I love my job!"

The phrase "Not Somehow, but Triumphantly" belongs to me, they say. But not as a boast of achievement; rather as a reminder of resources in Christ. I hope they remember that the word "triumph" implies a battle. It has not always been smooth sailing. I have needed all the grace my faith could grasp.

Their Gift to Me

(Looking back, this 50th anniversary of the Church of the Nazarene [1958], taking stock, a "pioneer"—rather, a "daughter of pioneers"—I see a holiness church as a gift to me, God's gift and theirs, those real pioneers! I see it as a gift of life's highest values.)

They gave me in my early teens my *summum bonum:* a personal relationship with God as the chief thing in life—Sundays, holidays, and every day; work and recreation; doing, talking, and thinking. Love God with all your heart, mind, soul, and strength; then love for neighbor follows—and there's not much room for anything else (Mark 12:30-31).

They gave me the doctrine of holiness, expounded by clear-thinking preachers—Bible-grounded, essential. "Any other gospel" was fatally less than the truth. Holiness of heart and life became an inwrought conviction determining life's most crucial choices; heart fellowship with another was unthinkable apart from agreement in this all-outness for God. "Can two walk together, except they be agreed?" (Amos 3:3; cf. 1 Pet. 1:15-16).

They gave me early the standard of *basic loyalty to the will of God.* A holy life is demanding, rigorous. No place for weak compromising. Righteousness means conviction to die for if necessary, to be lived in right habits. With Christ one can walk alone—safely. This, I learned, is the secret of holiness: a personal relationship with Jesus Christ (Matt. 10:38; 16:24-25).

They gave me the experience of *holiness as a living thing* —reality, truth, joy. The older people testified that it was "good to live in Canaan, where grapes of Eschol grow," and "better farther on." Their witness was attractive, their warmth of spirit compelling. They provided a norm by which to test all religious substitutes and detect the counterfeit. When I attended a secular college, I did not follow "wandering stars" nor "vain philosophies" (Jude 13; Col. 2:8).

They gave me *preparation* for the days when I had to walk alone. Standards that I followed by dead reckoning, because the best Christians I knew had held them, I learned later were based on sound principles—social, aesthetic, and moral as well as scriptural. They did not major on minors (John 14:6).

They gave me *protection.* "When my father and my mother forsake me, then the Lord will take me up." When my mother died and my father was unable to help me, then the

144

Lord's people mothered me. They taught me the meaning of the "family of God," "the household of faith," "Christian fellowship." They helped me to find a personal experience of my own, counseled me wisely, gave me responsibilities in the church that served as an anchor. They loved me away from Satan's lures (Ps. 27:10; Eph. 2:19; Acts 2:42).

They set before me the *pioneer pattern*. They lived before me the faith that takes dares for God. It seemed only natural to step out into the will of God, to accept His particular assignment for me, to strike out a new path, banking on His good faith. No money, no chart; but no fear, no question—in "our church" one doesn't live for self! (Gen. 12:1; Heb. 11:24-27).

*   *   *

Thank God for a church that gave me values that are permanent. May I be faithful in passing them on "to the generation following" (Ps. 48:13-14).

Success

Your conquering power you gain from Me. There can be no failure with Me. The secret of success then is life with Me.

Do you want to make the best of life? Then live very near to Me, the Master and Giver of all life. Your reward will be sure. It will be perfect success, but My success.

Sometimes the success of souls won, sometimes the success of disease cured, and devils cast out. Sometimes the success of a finished sacrifice as on Calvary. Sometimes the success of One who never answered a word in the face of the scorn and torture and jeering cries of His enemies, or the success of a Risen Savior as He walked through the garden of Joseph of Arimathea on that first Easter morning.

But My success. The world judges not as I judge. Bend your knees in wonder before My revelation. The joy of seeing spiritual truths is a great joy, when the heavens are opened and the Voice speaks to the faithful, loving heart.

6

Mini-Devotionals

Shining Pathway

The entire lake is a glow of palest rose of dawn; the hills beyond are half veiled in soft-tinted mists. The world is waking; the rose is fading; but the gold is brightening. The sun is sending its glory just to me. And my heart leaps with the reminder: *"Unto you . . . shall the Sun of righteousness arise."*

Then I remember that the same path of gold comes straight to the cottage around the bend. The world's sun, but a path to every individual.

> *Lord of all being, throned afar,*
> *Thy glory flames from sun and star;*
> . . . .
> *Yet to each loving heart how near!*

To the least of His children—to me. Thank God for the day I opened my life to the Light of the World. I would help other shuttered lives welcome the divine invasion.

I have called thee by thy name; thou art mine (Isa. 43:1).

On Wings

A pigeon flies into the road ahead and disappears beyond the hood of the car. Involuntarily I slow down cautiously, then laugh at myself: "Hard to run over a bird. He has wings." Then, "A Christian too has wings!" A Christian is never "caught" by circumstances.

Faith—The film unreels before my mind. That definitive picture of the bird who, "Pausing in his flight, / Rests on a

149

bough too slight, / And feeling it give way beneath him, sings, / Knowing he has wings." Earth may cave in under faith; but faith has heaven.

Strength—The mother eagle pushes her fledgling from the nest, still flies underneath to catch him should his wings fail—till finally those wings grow stronger than any gale. I feel the inflow of strength, sure and adequate. Above the storm into God's own sunlight!

They that wait upon the Lord shall renew their strength; they shall mount up with wings as eagles (Isa. 40:31).

Open-ended Above

Our sense of wonder dulls quickly. The wonder of grace must not evaporate in words. What we call "devotions" is our one open window to the skies. Daily as we keep the channel of communication unblocked, we shall learn to *live* the miracle, practice breathing eternity's atmosphere. Three phrases will help us grow in this grace.

(1) "According to the power that worketh in us." The wonder-working dynamic of the new creation is still ours. (2) "Bought with a price." The cost of this power was the death of the Son of God. We are not our own, but His. (3) "Without me . . . nothing," Jesus said. But with Him the force of endless life flows through you, through me, as sap through the vine's branches. It is this Person-to-person relationship that will keep us "open-ended above."

I can do all things through Christ which strengtheneth me (Phil. 4:13).

Stop on the Threshold

"When ye pray, say . . . *Father.*" Stop as you begin the morning prayer. Stop to recognize the wonder of your adoption—what a privilege and confidence, what love and understanding! Check on the relationship; make sure there is no break. Stop to realize and trust.

"When ye pray, say, *Our.*" Stop to remember the "whole family in heaven and earth." Feel the lift of those older brothers and sisters whose faith has helped you; the pull of those younger ones who need your faith; the tug of those potential, straying ones whom you must seek to bring home. Your relations with them are vital to your relations with the Father.

"Which art in heaven." Stop for fresh contact with the Father's home—that world of other laws and higher values. Stop to be lifted. Let the wind of heaven blow through your spirit.

Ye have received the Spirit of adoption, whereby we cry, Abba, Father (Rom. 8:15).

In the Audience Chamber

The threshold has expanded; you find yourself in the audience chamber of the King. Here the prayer of petition is possible. His scepter is extended.

The motivation of your prayer? *Thy kingdom come.* No self-centeredness here. If I am to ask "in Jesus' name," it is for His interests I am first concerned. Yet, "If children, then heirs"—heirs to the Kingdom. Wise to center all our prayers in what is to be our eternal possession.

The scope and authority of our prayer? Stop once again: *Thy will be done.* Whatever of detailed request, for self or for others, this is its frame. Here is essential good. Here you may "ask what ye will, and it shall be done." And the Spirit will suggest large asking, in this setting.

Hitherto have ye asked nothing in my name: ask, and ye shall receive, that your joy may be full (John 16:24).

Your Goings Out

Robert Louis Stevenson, in an essay extolling the merits of the venturesome life, called it a dangerous act to get out of bed in the morning; there are numberless ways you might be killed during the day. But, he asks, who wants to "hoard his life like a miser"? Some Christians are just that nearsighted, staying in bed spiritually, taking care of their own "experience."

Jesus says, "Out of bed and into the world"—a world full of need of Him. Go out to men in caring, in understanding, in love and sympathy; don't stay shut up in yourself and your own interests, even "religious" interests. "Go out" to find and bring to Jesus. Paul says he himself was pulled out by the love of Christ. His love for Christ? Christ's love for him? Both.

The love of Christ constraineth us (2 Cor. 5:14).

And Comings In

Go out, perhaps not very far, to bring in. Andrew brought his own brother; the "good" Samaritan brought a fellow traveler.

Go out to recommend, and live, the cure you have found for sin and sorrow. Those with hidden needs are watching—it may be, waiting—for your testimony.

Go out in prayer to lift, soul upraised for them in intercession until they are ready to lift their own. Go out in response: to every suggestion of the Spirit, to every responsibility of every relationship. Go out in gap-filling readiness.

"Your goings out"—for every one there will be a "coming in." The glorious promise is that these all shall be "preserved." God is not a Waster. He will not waste a consecrated life, nor a fraction of it.

The Lord shall preserve thy going out and thy coming in from this time forth (Ps. 121:8).

First Thoughts

What are your morning "firsts"? Alarm clock? Coffee? A mood? A problem? Rush? I have a secret for sneaking in early a thought of God that steals no time from the busy schedule —rather, will save time by oiling inevitable tensions and unifying random drives.

God understands that I have trusted Him to set the pattern of my day before the distractions set in—even before the set "devotions." Sometimes it comes with the sudden key to an elusive problem of the previous evening, stirring thanksgiving for His attention to my specific "secular" interests; sometimes with the verse of scripture that He knows speaks to my condition, or will so speak; or with the name of a person in special need of my prayer. And, often, with a song that takes over for the day, making melody to Him in my heart.

Bringing into captivity every thought to the obedience of Christ (2 Cor. 10:5).

153

"Lo" and "Behold"!

Look, and see! A glad wonder of surprise. Not He *will* be here; He *is*. "Lo, I *am* with you . . . unto the end." With that "Lo" the voice of God is shattering our sleepy preoccupation: Wake up! Open your eyes! See!

Lo, "this woman . . . whom Satan hath bound." She lives next door to you. You pass her in the street. But you had not really seen her. Look! You know the Christ who breaks fetters.

"Lo, Sarah thy wife shall have a son." You too have stepped out on a promise but have found yourself ending up in a blind alley. But, lo, a door is opening in the blank wall before you! Faith sees a faithful God still at work on your problem.

"Behold, I am with thee." Of course your mountain assignment is too much for you. But behold! the mighty God is by your side! God's "Behold!" is Siamese twin to His "Go!"

I will send thee . . . Certainly I will be with thee (Exod. 3:10, 12).

The Golden Rule

The Golden Rule—the one law that everybody admires, praises—and neglects. The one everyone wishes the other fellow would follow. Jesus rated it high.

"Thou shalt love thy neighbour" in *deeds*. Act justly; act helpfully; push him ahead when you see, or can make, an opportunity.

154

"Thou shalt love thy neighbour" in *words*. Speak honestly; let him know that he can depend on your word. Speak strongly; dare tell the truth to him when others would tell it about him. And be silent strongly; listen to his secrets and bury them. Speak kindly: *to* him when his heart is sore, *of* him when others would laugh at his expense. A good name is worth more than millions—don't be a thief.

Owe no man any thing, but to love one another ... Love is the fulfilling of the law (Rom. 13:8, 10).

The Gift of Laughter

Laughter is God's good gift to man. And in a peculiar sense only His victorious children know the joy of pure laughter. Even in the midst of persecution we can be "absurdly happy," as one has expressed it. "We know sorrow, yet our joy is inextinguishable" (2 Cor. 6:10, Phillips).

"There is . . . a time to laugh." You catch yourself inordinately concerned over something mosquito-sized; you can laugh. Thank God for the gift of humor. To be able to laugh at oneself is to have a true sense of relative values. The talent deserves to be cultivated.

God's gift of a pure heart brings with it the "mirth that has no bitter springs." It could be clouded or blotted out by suspicion or sophistication or discontent. Guard it well. "If you cannot do anything else for Christ, you can be happy for Him" (A. B. Simpson). Your joy will attract others.

Rejoice in the Lord alway: and again I say, Rejoice (Phil. 4:4).

Personally Conducted Tour

Any place Christ takes us is worth visiting. *The valley of refreshing,* of course. "Beside the still waters. He restoreth my soul." *The field of routine* glorified; the yoke is fitted, and He walks beside the plow. *The fishing expedition:* "Follow me, and I will make you fishers." A nightlong vigil and empty nets, but in the morning His command, "Launch out into the deep"—and the "multitude of fishes."

The wilderness. "Then was Jesus led up of the Spirit . . . to be tempted of the devil." The One who went this way before is whispering strength and pointing the path to the exit. The "valley of the shadow" and the *deep waters of affliction.* Still He is at our side, holding back the flooded rivers. In the darkness we feel His strong arm and hear His "Fear not."

Fear thou not; for I am with thee: be not dismayed; for I am thy God (Isa. 41:10).

7

Letters
to Students

April 25, 1975 (in her 88th year)
Dear Earl,

I'm obeying the inner voice again. And the voice of "my pastor." You said to get this pledge card in by the third day. This is the second day since I heard that advice.

As tithes and offerings are already committed, this must be a special thank-offering—very small for the rich food I am receiving and enjoying. It comes with a prayer and trust that God will follow it—direct it week by week to some hungry heart, perhaps on the other side of the world.

And now my testimony. I am following closely the Vine and the Branches. I feel a deep earnestness in your voice—and His. Especially this morning the reminder that the Spirit bears the fruit . . .

I'll share F. R. Havergal:

> He is with thee! In thy service.
> He is with thee certainly!
> Filling with the Spirit's power,
> Giving in the needing hour
> His own messages by thee.
> He is with thee! With thy spirit,
> With thy lips and with thy pen;
> In the heart-bowed congregation,
> Nevermore alone again.

Those last words (my underlining) have gripped me for my special needs at this time.

Yours and His,
BERTHA MUNRO

March 11, 1975
Dear Hazel:

Always when I write to Earl I feel I am writing to you also, but this morning I'm addressing you alone because I've been filling his mailbox with words from me, and I'm embarrassed to add another so soon. Yet I have something I want him to know, and I thought you could get it to him sometime unobtrusively.

You see, I'm listening greedily to his sermons these days. This morning it was February 23, "Open My Eyes . . . to Singing"—a totally new presentation of truth, but so true to my experience that I believe I should share it with him (I notice he said this morning that this sort of sharing brings him pleasure).

You see, I have no voice for singing. In high school the singing teacher tested us individually and dismissed me, saying, "You can't even sing the scale." I can murmur along with the rest, and I do, and love it. By this time I know all the songs, word for word, every verse. It's not only the sound but the meaning—I think by a sort of compensation so much of my treasured truth has come to me and stayed with me in those words, all coming out of the experience of men and women who knew God.

Well, about two years or more ago I realized one day that for several mornings I had found myself when I came to consciousness singing—in my heart and mind—the words of a gospel song. And I recalled that my Mary Harris had several times asked the Lord for a song. So I asked Him if He could not continue this, and every morning let me wake up singing. (The song had always set my mood for the day and many times directed my mind to some person or action that proved to be His thought for me, His will.)

This He has done for me, through me, every day since, and how I thank Him. A very few days—I would say four or five—it wasn't there at first. But "Lord, where is my song?" It came at once, without my conscious choice.

This has been wonderful to me—I'm sure it has been His loving way of making up to me for my lack of the means of

160

praising Him in song. It hasn't taken the place of the Bible in my life but has tightened my fellowship with Him.

Thanks for listening,
BERTHA MUNRO

March 24, 1976
Dear Earl:

What a joy your latest letter! Specially to hear that you were "getting concerned" because I wasn't keeping up the schedule. I had been trying to give you a little rest—I knew I was taking more than my share of your time.

Finding you and Hazel now is God's own gift to me in these years—finding a depth of harmony existing that I cannot describe. I can share things with you as I cannot with anyone else [probably because of the freedom of expression in letters] and feel that you will understand and really listen. But I must trust you to be honest—that is a friend's duty.

When you have the slightest feeling that I am overstepping in any way, and/or the Spirit gives a check—but of course you would obey that—be sure to tell me. Otherwise I couldn't be free.

*　　*　　*

Office of the Dean Emeritus
May 19, 1975
Dear Earl:

On tiptoe with joy! All morning it's been singing itself over in my mind—or heart—whatever. Oh, yes, Dr. Seamands' *On Tiptoe with Joy!* You see, I was up to date with the 1975 tapes and was doing a repeat, back to January, and your recipe for the year—

. . . It is gratitude I feel to you, of course, for showing us the way, but beyond that, to the God whose name is I AM,

161

with all that means; utterly faithful, beyond all measure—above all we ask or think.

And this *joy:* the clear-cut denomination of what "total commitment" means and how it operates. Behind your recall vote I seem to see months of a vision of God's will laid hold of by faith and kept alive for weeks and days of commitment reaffirmed by trusting obedience—hard work and joy in the constant day-by-day strengthening. And with that I keep hearing Hazel's "point of no return" and know the contact with heaven was always kept open, and "two were agreeing."

Another joy: I heard you read the "Great Joy" verses and remembered how in sending them to Dr. Purkiser [then editor of the *Herald of Holiness*] I had been compelled by the feeling (quenching all modesty) that I wish I could shout them to the entire church. It came to me when you had finished reading, that, as usual, God was giving more: through the tapes the shout was reaching the whole world!

I'm truly grateful that "we are one in the bond of love."

As always,
BERTHA MUNRO

July 29, 1976
St. Albans, Vt.
Dear Earl:

I had a great day yesterday . . . time to watch a glorious deep rose sunset with dark edges—darkness slowly taking over as the sun went down—the whole a beautiful *afterglow* that spoke to me of a closing life—with just the God-contact (conversation) I know was meant for me.

At 10 P.M. I listened on TV to the history of Mars and continued with the double-crostic puzzle I was working on. Once I start one the challenge of the puzzle takes over, especially at a certain point.

So after a cup of chocolate with Mars, I continued with the puzzle. At 12:15, with only a few critical spots not filled—the last 15 minutes in bed—I exerted self-discipline and turned out the light, thanking God for a perfect day—thoroughly rested, and slept all night.

So this morning, after my songs and my talk with the Lord about them, I was surprised when He said, "You must write Earl about this." So here it is:

Jesus denied himself: He lived in the Father's will, not His own; He came not to do His own thing—which is what the younger generation claim when they say they want to be themselves—"I want to find myself."

On the Cross Jesus' seven words express a basic aspect of the truly beautiful, normal life—no more, no less:

1) physical need (disciplined)
2) care for family and friend
3) forgiveness of enemies
4) desire to save the lost
5) agony at temporary hiding of the Father's face
6) faithful completion of an assigned task
7) final commitment with trust to God at death

In Him,
BERTHA MUNRO

April 4, 1977

Dear Earl:

A blessed Easter to you!

I know this Easter dawn will speak great things to you—an eternal freshness in the Resurrection *story*—no, *fact*. "Story" does not seem quite strong enough for what I feel.

I must tell you about my Easter. For three days, last Thursday, Friday, and Saturday—I had a very clear answer to

a desperate prayer . . . as to my attitude, to speak or be silent
. . . well, early in the morning, as usual:

> Thursday it was Faith, naked faith.
> Friday it was Joy, His joy (in the face of the Cross
> ahead).
> Saturday it was self-giving, total.

And then I knew I could look ahead—only then—to
Sunday. *Resurrection.*

I found myself asking, Is it really so? That someday I
shall stop breathing here and the next minute be breathing
another atmosphere—seeing the dawn of a new sunrise?

It seemed so very real—that wonderful Easter morning.
That sequence was like Jesus' last days:

> *Naked Faith—a face set to go to Jerusalem*
> *His joy that He promised His disciples*
> *The total giving of Gethsemane and Calvary—*
> *and then Resurrection.*

It is the way the Master went;
May (Should) the disciple tread it still?

A blessed Easter of loving and giving and fullness of joy.
My love and prayers and faith.

Thank you for listening,
BERTHA MUNRO

March 24, 1976

"I . . . know" nothing "save Jesus Christ, and him crucified."

I was thinking this morning back to my own experience.
At four crises where I came face-to-face with death, always
the Spirit brought Jesus to me:

1) When I was 15 years old and they brought me the
message that my mother had died, these words came
to my mind (I must have read them before but not

noticed): "They shall see his face; and *his name* shall be on [sic] their foreheads."

2) When I was 24 and pinned under the wreckage of a railroad train, facedown, in the dark, and thought it was the end of life, the words of a song, new to me then, came singing,

> *Jesus, oh, how sweet the name,*
> *Jesus, every day the same.*

3) When I was 40, and my father was dying—I had prayed all night (he had suffered a stroke the morning before and had been in a coma since—his last hours now) that I might have some assurance of his relation to God. He "came to" at about 10 A.M. and I read some of John 14 and asked him what I should sing. Just two words came: "Jesus"—"stranger."

   "Do you mean Jesus sought me when a stranger?"

   "It's true," he said.

4) In 1969 (I was 82) Mary Harris—very shortly before she died—had me "sing" softly with her, "Through the gates to the city . . . But I long to meet my Saviour first of all." And the first thing I was aware of May 10 was that Jesus was welcoming her through the gates. Twenty minutes later a phone call told me she had gone.

Add to this the time I began my real scholar-wise *thinking,* the day I heard a lecturer say, "The greatest single event in all history (not theology) was the crucifixion of Jesus Christ." I said to myself, "That's true. And if so—all my value judgments—philosophical, literary—dealing with man, his nature, his needs, must be made in the light of that basic fact."

Jesus Christ has been, and is, central in my thinking.

And the latest word I have been facing is "total identification" with Jesus as the meaning of entire sanctification.

165

"God will never answer our prayer to be baptized with the Holy Spirit for any other reason than to be a witness for Jesus."

*   *   *

May 1, 1980

Dear Ones:

Last night I could not sleep, and I knew I must write to you. I feel so keenly with you and for you. For Gary, of course—I know how much he means to you.

But now more—to understand the ways of God. My heart aches for you.

This is a "Job experience." Job made it through, and I know you will. But the end of the agonizing experience has not come—my prayers are with you. And my

Lasting love,

BERTHA MUNRO

(EDITOR'S NOTE: This was Dean Munro's last note to Dr. and Mrs. Earl G. Lee, whose son Gary was at that time one of the American hostages imprisoned in Iran. This note of concern "was written . . . in a frail handwriting as delicate as a spider's web.")

8

Poetry

Gifts

The wise men came, that far-off winter dawn,
And brought their gifts—gold, myrrh, and frankincense—
To Christ, the King. But as they turned to go,
Their pathway changed into a road of gold,
A heavenly fragrance to their garments clung,
And songs of praise set all the world aflame.
Blessing the King, themselves were blessed indeed.
I, too, brought treasures to my Lord divine.
I brought my gold—my wealth of human joys,
My friends, my gathered store of truth, my work.
I brought my myrrh, the bitter griefs of years;
And frankincense, the worship of my heart.
I brought them to His feet, and laid them there.
But, lo, He touched my gifts, and gave them back
Radiant, transformed, a royal gift to me.
His joy transmuted mine to living gold,
Gave my frail work pledge of eternity;
His peace breathed on my griefs, and perfumes rare
Of sympathy and faith and hope distilled;
His love on my soul's altar kindled there
An answering flame, and showed my Savior's face.
In the King's hands poor gifts wax infinite.

"Thanks Be unto God for His Unspeakable Gift"

He gave me Light:
   The light of those upon whose darkness dawns
   A strong, sure ray. Sitting in helpless night
   And shadow of death, on me the glory shone.

He gave me Joy:
   The joy of those whose mouth is sudden filled
   With singing laughter and a glad surprise;
   The joy of heaven's wells for each day's need.

He gave me Peace:
   The peace of those who find calm after storm,
   And rest, deep-centered, 'mid life's grinding cares.

He gave me Truth:
   The highest thing a soul may know on earth,
   Glimpse of a universe of sun and star
   Gladly obeying God's all-perfect will;
   My heart, with them, transparent, unafraid.

He gave me Love:
   Filling my emptiness, healing every hurt,
   Binding all broken things, and reaching out
   To suffering, groping millions, to fulfill
   Itself by being spilt—His love, not mine.

   This Thou hast given—this to me, O Lord?
   This Thou hast given, for Thou gavest thyself;
   Traveled the road, the road thyself didst make—
   From glory to my need, from God to me.
   O Gift unspeakable—thyself—to me!

Epiphany

To wise men from the wary ways of thought,
  Searchers for truth, following the beckoning gleam
A light shone from the manger, and His face.
  No seeking more, but ever rest in Him!
    He is the Truth.
To Saul of Tarsus, toiling in the right,
  Serving indeed, but with no God to know,
A Light, a Voice laid claim. "What wilt Thou, Lord?"
  "My name is Love. Serve Me with heart aglow.
    I am the Way."
To sinners, hopeless, impotent, and dead,
  Once more the Christ appears in living light.
He breaks the spell of failure and regret,
  He shines in power and everlasting might.
    He is the Life.
Epiphany—my Lord, the Christ revealed!
My Truth, my Way, my Life, for aye unveiled.

As He Said

Not fettered in the dark, cold tomb my Lord,
But risen! risen! The trembling Easter dawn
Swells to a sea of light. My Lord is risen!
Risen, as He said. And now He goes before.
Tracing His steps—my Sun no more goes down—
I walk the path that shines yet more and more
To perfect day. I serve the living Christ.

Not orphaned in a world of chance and change.
The night of sin and wrong shall yet become
The radiant morn of heaven. My Lord is coming!
Coming, as He said. On those glad hills of light
Beyond the blue, the clock of God still strikes
Unerringly. And constant to His word,
My Lord will come. I shall behold His face.

Great Joy

All heaven was singing, and the joy spilled over;
   The angels knew the wonder of His birth.
The joy of heaven, tumultuous, deep and holy,
   Then burst upon the weary, waiting earth.

That strange, new joy this world had never dreamed of,
   The joy to heal its age-old bitter smart.
It winged the feet of lowly men believing;
   It whispered in the brooding mother's heart.

That joy of heaven once given, abides among us;
   It sings amid the shadows of the tomb;
It lifts the shout of Resurrection morning,
   Its magic finds a glory in the gloom.

That joy—blest overflow of heaven's hosannas—
   Still overfills our hungry human want;
That song still echoes till its swells,
     returning,
    Eternity's Alleluia chant.

9

Other Writings

The Ancient Beautiful Things

Surrounded by the restless spirit of change, in a day impatient of tradition and snatching everything modern, we could let slip some ancient, beautiful, God-given treasures.

The first of these is the Giver himself. Today let me be quiet to see the King in His beauty, the Ancient of Days, and to worship the Lord in the beauty of holiness.

The two most beautiful of the ancient things, the philosopher Kant said, are "the starry heavens above and the moral law within." Beautiful and abiding, and both equally for our delight—the law of God in nature around us, the law of God in our own natures! Not to be rightly adjusted to His will is ugliness and discord.

Dorothy Thompson, writing in 1952, summed up the true "American way of life" in terms of two ancient beautiful things of her youth that she fears we might lose. They are more than American; they go back to creation's dawn, fresh from the hand of God. One she calls "the most human standard of life and relationships: hard work."

You didn't think it beautiful, the joy of achievement? the opportunity to create, most of all to create strong, useful character, in the image of God, the Worker, Creator?

The other factor of the "American way" named—this too as ancient as God's first revelation—is "lovingness, pulling people up instead of pushing them down . . . belonging to a nation of friends and doing as you would be done by." The Golden Rule is an ancient beautiful thing—forever new. If we make it ours, day in, day out.

Home is an ancient beautiful thing. Like all the others, it has been sanctioned and ordained by the Father in heaven; it is kept beautiful by following His specifications and living in His Spirit. Every Christian—though the actual family circle may not be complete—should find some way to create the atmosphere of home wherever he is. It is his right.

Fatherhood, in the flesh or in the spirit, its privileges and responsibilities: giving the world a reproduction of oneself, one's life extended to another generation, walking for another to follow one's steps, providing, protecting, shielding; motherhood and wifehood with their self-forgetful giving out; the art of being a brother or a son—all these can be cheapened. Some of them have been travestied, smirched by ugly living and uglier psychopathic fads. We need to keep them beautiful. God's Word shows us the way.

Friendship is an ancient, beautiful thing. And neighborliness. Beautiful if they follow the pattern of Jonathan and the Good Samaritan: treasures found by giving.

So it is of all these beautiful things that have lasted. They pull the best out of us, and so give back the best. I shall make my world better by cultivating them.

The Bible

**O how love I thy law! it is my meditation
all the day** (Ps. 119:97).

For ever, O Lord, thy word is settled in heaven (Ps. 119:89).

The Word of God is eternal as God is eternal, for it represents His character. The truth expressed in it is wrought into the fabric of our moral universe. Useless to try to evade the Ten Commandments or to bypass the Atonement. They are demands of our nature. Suicidal to believe the tempter when he whispers that the promise will fail, or that there is some better way than the law of love.

The Bible is proved and provable. Look back on the day when you obeyed its command to repent and trusted its promise of salvation; you proved with David that God brings up out of the depths, lifts from horrible pit to solid rock, puts a song in the mouth.

Remember the many days when you almost went under, but you trusted the promise for strength as the day, and proved with Isaiah that "they that wait upon the Lord shall renew their strength," and with Paul that "grace is sufficient."

When the new testing comes and you face the overwhelming emergency, remember the cloud of witnesses, those centuries of men and women who have proved that not one word has failed. And as life shatters one human ideal after another, prove with deep thanksgiving that you never can be disappointed in the God of the Bible.

"Heaven and earth shall pass away, but my words shall not pass away."

Channels, Not Cisterns

He that believeth on me . . . out of his belly shall flow rivers of living water. (But this spake he of the Spirit, which they that believe on him should receive . . .) (John 7:38-39).

Strange words, but in this connection, attention demanding. They are Jesus' words, announcing publicly the new pattern for His followers, of life in the Spirit. They are spoken in parable language, as usual.

The true Christian life is not a *cistern,* to guard a sanctified experience; rather, a *channel* for the free course of the Holy Spirit, in a stream of ever-fresh living water, to be shared with others. Remember the prophet's healing waters (Ezekiel 47) and John's pure river of life (Rev. 22:1).

No strain here. Our "witness" is a life lived in daily fellowship and obedience. Our one responsibility is to keep both inflow and outflow points unclogged. Those points are clearly defined; no hindrance is allowed.

Here is a love service that does not cease with advancing years. The apparent size of the opening may vary with the means of grace available and the evangelistic outreach possible. For both there is always prayer, and eyes for opportunities.

Changed

We shall all be changed! Paul's exultant affirmation—Handel's ringing trumpet echo—God's promise is sure. "In a moment"! "I know . . . at the last day." "Like him; for we shall see him as he is."

But now? The "shall . . . be" disturbs me. Every "shall be" of divine promise has its "shall be" of human cooperation. Now, "the mind of Christ."

Is prayer subjective or objective? Changing us or changing the world? Both. "It is the man who shares My life and whose life I share that proves fruitful." "Apart from me . . . nothing." "If you live your life in me, . . . ask for whatever you like" (Phillips). Achievement in prayer is conditioned on identification with Christ; and identification comes through prayer.

"Take time." Why? Sharing takes time. Time to open ourselves wide to His thinking, His spirit, His purposes.

We come to prayer from the clamor of this noisy world. We stay until perspective is trued and we see from Christ's point of view. Until vision is enlarged; shut in with our petty concerns, we had not realized there were so many, such over-whelming needs. Until we see Christ dying for us. Until we are compelled to *ask*.

Stay until vision is *focused* on what He is interested in getting done just now. Until, with a bit of His wisdom, we are ready to ask *in His name*. Until desire is kindled, intensified; until, with some small sharing of His love, we can ask with urgency that receives—"what things soever ye *desire*."

And not spasmodically, sporadically, but today, tomor-row, and tomorrow's tomorrow, until *fellowship* is developed, and faith has become habit and a mountain a challenge.

"Ask," He says; "ask largely." Ask with confidence. Ask with desire enough to do something. Ask with the power of sincerity, caring as He cares.

Take time to be changed—by sharing.

The Risen Christ Recognized

Luke 24:28-35

He was known of them in breaking of bread (Luke 24:35).

Christ still is to be invited in. We who have met Him face-to-face can sing, "He lives within my heart," and know its meaning. We have the confidence of His constant pres-ence, strengthening, and guiding. But how often we could enjoy the consciousness of that presence in personal fellow-ship if we could set ourselves to entertain Him! A glimpse then, and He was gone. Since Pentecost He stays with us by His Spirit. He is always available.

Jesus is Blesser, Giver—always. We think we give Him bread. We put our common lives gladly in His hands. But He gives them back, readied for service, with His blessing—now rich, holy things because He has touched them. We need offer Him no grand feast; it is our ordinary selves, our ordinary living, that He shines through.

Christ lives. His resurrection is, historically, the best-authenticated fact about Him. Doubly authenticated when re-proved in you and me. This the master clue that fits together all life's jumbled pieces. It clears our minds and satisfies our hearts. It relates us personally to Jesus Christ, and through Him to the Father and to all men. With those first disciples we say, "My Lord and my God."

Good News of Peace

Luke 2:8-20

Behold, I bring you good tidings of great joy, which shall be to all people (Luke 2:10).

And now excitement on earth! News scoop of all the ages! Inside story given to the shepherds and spread by them. "Too good to keep"—they set us a pattern. The gospel is always a scoop, if we could remember.

The news is good, the joy is great—small wonder, for it is heaven let down to earth. We are a God-visited planet. Forever hereafter there will be a kingdom of heaven among us and of us.

> *Joy to the world! the Lord is come;*
> *Let earth receive her King.*

The best of it is that the news is provable individually. "O come, all ye faithful, joyful and triumphant." "Let us go . . . and see." So it is still: They heard and saw, as it was told them; "they came . . . and found . . . [and] made known"; they returned, praising and telling the message of peace and good

180

will. Gospel provers are peace-finders, peace-spreaders—
peacemakers, for the kingdom of God is within them. They
have an inexhaustible supply, independent of wars and rumors of wars. They are blessed and blessing.

> He comes to make His blessings flow
> Far as the curse is found.

We will share our good news.

A New Englander reminisces about . . .

Preaching in the Early Days of the Holiness Movement

Every sermon was doctrinal, biblical, largely expository, with
special application to the experience of holiness, to be received here and now. Holiness was preached both Sunday
morning and evening by the pastors, and by every evangelist
in every revival meeting and camp meeting. In "all-day meetings" also; almost every holiday was spent in these meetings
—morning, afternoon, and evening. In Massachusetts, April
19 and May 30 were the great days. We all attended as a
matter of course, children and all. My experience began at the
age of nine.

The doctrine of entire sanctification was found by some
preachers in texts that probably had to be wrenched from
context to apply to the experience. But the great, definite
proof texts were used over and over by all the sermon-
makers until we knew them by heart. The sermons were not
dead, however, nor boring—even to me, as a child. They
were full of life and living, and always directed at *me*.

There were powerful pulpiteers in those days, men of the finest educational background and training—Methodist ministers who had been sanctified after preaching some years, and for whom the experience marked an explosive crisis that had cost them everything. Dr. Daniel Steele (more writer than preacher) was a Boston University professor. Dr. C. J. Fowler had been a prominent figure in New England Methodism. Dr. Beverly Carradine and Dr. H. C. Morrison had similar standing in the South. There was the brilliant, warmhearted young Will Huff. Bud Robinson was a winsome natural genius. And other "greats"—we knew them all. Camp meetings brought South to all; North and West to East. We forgot that Texas claimed "Uncle Bud"; he belonged to us. Of course in those earlier days we had our preferences. Our favorite was Dr. Carradine. His vivid illustrations made us cry with pity and shiver with fear.

Some evangelists had their favorite message and favorite text. For Rev. Martha Curry, from Stoneham, Mass., self-educated, but a forceful personality and speaker, the theme was the *leprosy* of "inbred sin" and Naaman's dipping seven times in Jordan; or the trip of the Israelites from Egypt to Canaan (text: Deut. 6:23: "He brought us out from thence, that he might bring us in, to give us the land which he sware unto our fathers"). The Canaan image was universal. The language was well understood.

Another text of Miss Curry's that still rings in my ears was Titus 2:14. She always read from the beginning in verse 11, "The grace of God that bringeth salvation hath appeared," but she concentrated on verse 14: "Who gave himself for us, that he might redeem us from all iniquity, and purify unto himself a peculiar people, zealous of good works." And now as I think of it, that was not a bad text.

The total emphasis was always evangelistic. Only one preacher do I recall saying much about the "process" of growth; but even he made the "crisis" plain. That was Rev.

John Short, pastor formerly of a large Methodist church in Lowell, Mass. (our Wollaston church altar came from that church building), then for years pastor of the Cambridge Church of the Nazarene. We youngsters called him "Mr. Long," for obvious reasons—in those days an hour was exceptionally short for a sermon; his went much farther. His text, whether expounded or quoted, in every message was: "Nevertheless, whereto we have already attained, let us walk by the same rule, let us mind the same thing."

For the most part they trusted to "the experience," a sound case of the "second blessing, properly so-called," genuinely received and kept alive, to keep one going. They wanted us to "get it good." And they usually kept us digging until we found our way to the heart of things.

Their call was to "spread scriptural holiness." Pentecost, of course—Acts 2:4 was a must text and was preached again and again, but always qualified by Acts 15:8-9. The blessing was primarily for purity, not for power; for cleansing, not merely for "service." The power would be that purity. "Eradication" of the "carnal mind" was the terminology. We could repreach, or anticipate, step by step the outlines of what sanctification (1) was, (2) was not; (3) would not do, (4) would do.

Every sermon aimed, or was calculated, to make those present recognize a personal need, if one existed; a searching "test" was almost always given.

The altar service followed every sermon. And it was long. Seekers were expected to "pray through." The term was "entire consecration," not "commitment." (And not "surrender"—surrendering was for the sinner seeking forgiveness and "laying down his arms of rebellion.") The direction for the Christian seeking holiness was, "Die out." These preachers thought logically, exactly.

They were blazing a trail, and they wanted to blaze it straight and plain. They did!

10

A Collection of Gems

God will not waste a consecrated life.

My soul has felt the stir of the life that never ends.

God will always give the best to those who leave the choice to Him.

There is no conflict between the best in education and the best in the Christian faith.

God keeps His promises forever.

Every promise is a challenge to action.

It is what God will make of me that counts, not what I started with.

Truth will not bend to make the way easier for us.

No Siamese twins more closely joined than these: Trust and Obey.

To turn down a divine call is to rob God and to cheat yourself.

He who has found the Living Bread will not be seeking satisfaction in the world's garbage barrels.

A problem is an opportunity to prove God.

To be worldly is to live for time and sense rather than for eternity and God's program.

There's no finality in failure—unless you will it.

Faith in Christ is not an upside-down cone teetering tipsily on its point; faith in Christ is a pyramid resting firmly on its base, broadening down and settling surely so it cannot be overturned, more real and more precious than life.

I will not change the cut of my heavenly clothes to suit the fashions of an overnight lodging.

"No shoddy work or unsound timbers go into this boat," said Noah. "I have to float in it."

By our admissions or our alibis we are becoming strong men or shifty.

To be disloyal to the best we know is to make a poor bargain.

God cares less about our work for Him than about our relationship to Him.

Don't shrink yourself into a millionaire, if God told you to become a missionary.

Life's difficulties are not watered down to fit our ability. The problems are not given us already solved, nor even with answer appended.

It is human nature to justify self by shifting blame.

The only standard for us is our best for God and heaven.

Both money and friends will turn to ashes in your hands if you put them first in your planning.

I need to stop talking about prayer—and pray.

Faith can, if it chooses, laugh at the impossible.

Every Christian is at once put on display: a light set on a candlestick, a city set on a hill.

A hazy repentance means playing with sin; a hazy faith means playing with doubt.

Don't be afraid to spend money on God.

Faith must always stretch itself beyond sight.

Keep up-to-date in getting your assignments and directions.

Every prayer must be brought to the test of God's judgment.

I really believe God knows more than I do. That is why I trust His judgment on my problems.

Never risk asking God for anything without quickly adding, "If it be Thy will."

We should do more for God if we listened more.

There is an eternal Rock beneath a trusting soul.

Ask Him to give you a song in the morning and keep all your day to its melody.

It is well to live up-to-date in obedience, so that the next move is God's.

God's food makes you grow; your old diet was starving you.

Everyone should aim to make some contribution to his generation before he passes on. Life should not disappear like a bubble leaving no trace.

Prayer is not the easy waving of a magic wand. Prayer is helping God overthrow the forces of darkness.

Grace does not provide an escape from life but a conquest of life.

Our liberties are more than a possession; they are a trust.

God with us means that life has a *guiding star* and a sure destination.

Calvary—no one can know its depth of meaning, but all must reckon with it.

Grasp a promise of God and cling to it with all your might.

The best moral man is still of this world; each of us must enter the kingdom of God as "a little child."

There is a perfect plan of God for your life which you will never know unless you give Him the keys.

Whatever life's changes or surprises or perplexities, the things that cannot be shaken are yours.

You have something God needs and will use for His glory.

Because He knows we need Him above all else, He demands that we hold Him above all else.

It pays to stay within hearing distance of Jesus.

The bird with wings was made for the skies.

Anything that belongs to God is safe in His universe.

The Cross shows that we win by yielding, we rise by stooping, we are great by serving.

Faith is proved by obedience through the fog and the darkness.

God cannot be treated with casual politeness.

Your decisions and actions are based on convictions, not on convenience.

To be stingy with God's grace is to starve yourself as any miser does.

Don't take God for granted. He can safely double His blessings on a grateful person.

It is sheer foolishness not to team up with God in this business of running a life.

Trials make us sharers with Christ; He suffered.

If we could pierce the cloud, we should see the Father looking our way.

When you dress each day, do not forget to put on "the garment of praise."

It is much simpler to talk about good things than to live them.

Be sure that you do not make your longtime choices before you have met Jesus and asked His advice.

The song of triumph can ring in our hearts while we are in the thick of the fight.

The only way to insure our place in eternity is to qualify in time.

Look your alibis and excuses in the face, and you will find back of them some reluctance to yield your own will.

If only our hearts sing, the weight of the years is lifted.

As life shatters one human ideal after another, prove with deep thanksgiving that you can never be disappointed in the God of the Bible.

What Satan would use to destroy, God uses to develop.

With God there are no ordinary days.

You are most Christian when you are holding steady under pressure.

I am freest when I yield my will to Him.

If you lose your sky, you will soon lose your earth.

It is one thing to choose God's way; it is another thing—and a longer process—to learn God's way.

Christ has no favorites, but He fights on the side of the man who keeps His commandments.

A holy heart is not the end, but the beginning.

If you obey, there is nothing to fear; if you neglect, there is everything to fear.

The future is not a leap in the dark; the future is in our Father's hands.

No crisis has ever taken God by surprise—not even this crisis of yours!

Jesus always has specialized in transformed lives; no one is unpromising to Him.

A promise delayed is not a promise broken.

God does not stop working when things look hopeless.

The finest use any person can make of his life is to invest it somewhere in the service of Christ.

The life that has been touched by the presence of God bears the marks.

With God new needs spell new means.

I would rather be a builder than a wrecker any day.

The world is not big enough to satisfy one soul.

If the rough road draws us closer to our Shepherd, it is well worth traveling.

When He seems to delay too long, He is not making a mistake. . . . He knows what He is doing.

Sometimes it is easier to say that big "Yes" in the initial step of faith than to keep saying the small "Yeses" along the way.

Faith wears everyday clothes and proves herself in life's ordinary situations.

It amounts to atheism to have a God, then live as if there were no God.

God does not have to have perfect stuff to make His saints out of.

If sin is a light thing, why the Cross?

If you don't want to pay much for your religion, you'll get a poor brand.

A Christian life is not built by rigid rule; it must be flexible in the hands of Christ.

The man who has followed God's directions in prosperity is safe in adversity.

For every bit of ground I help another possess, a foot or so is added to my own acreage.

A crack of half an inch could have sunk the ark.

Salvation is not buying cheap an entrance to heaven; salvation is having something done to me. Jesus must do it— but we must let Him have us to work on.

I don't expect God to pass my examinations for me when I have been too lazy to study.

To Calvary I pin my faith forever.

Monday to Saturday is the test of Sunday.

Let Jesus carry your hurts as well as your sins.

Jesus specializes in hard cases and impossible sinners.

Do not let your nice words come from the teeth out.

Your Christian life is not secondhand; others can show you the way, but you and God must make it together.

The bitterest test of faith is the test of waiting.

When we have no homes or goods we can still keep open house in our hearts.

Christians are not expected to muddle through. They are expected to face life head-on and triumph.

Every ordinary day given to God and touched by God is a sacrament.

The joy of the Lord is not an uninterrupted grin.

There is no dead-end street for the true wayfaring Christian.

The call to utmost dependence on God is also a call to utmost human effort.

When God appointed us, He took on the burden of our support.

With God it is always quality first, not quantity; spirit, not achievement; motive, not deed.

192

There is no panic in trust.

The narrow way leads straight up the hill.

Faith sees a faithful God still at work on our problem.

Prepare for Jesus' return by obeying, not by gazing.

Whatever pulls you away from God is for you worldly.

I cannot wait for an emergency to learn to pray.

To dodge the issue is not to settle it.

Afflictions as well as successes will drive us forward in the plan of God, if our sails are set right.

If your religion is pale, colorless, lukewarm, you have been cheated into taking a substitute.

No trial can reach you without God's permission, and God's notice—or without God's way through and out.

The vision comes to those whose eyes are open.

Don't let yourself grow careless or slovenly. Keep dressed for the Bridegroom's coming.

Wisdom is planning a life in the will of God.

I cannot see the turns of the road ahead; but I know I shall find Him at every one.

When we choose to obey God without reserve we are not taking a leap in the dark; we are trusting ourselves to a Person we know. And what a Person!

The mountain of problems that confronts you at this moment—give it by an act of the will to Jesus.

God is not willing that any should perish—and He has plenty of lifeboats.

11

The Bible
as
Literature

Above all, Bertha Munro was a Christian teacher. Of her teaching, a student of the 1950s writes, "Majoring in literature under Dean Munro and sitting in her Sunday School class benefited me mentally and spiritually far beyond what I can tell you. It was she who believed that I could be a teacher and gave me the self-confidence to attempt it. I will soon retire from teaching, but I will thank God for a lifetime for Dean Munro."

This book, which bears the title *The Best of Bertha Munro*, would not be complete without the inclusion of an example of her superb teaching. Out of a firm grounding in literature, coupled with her Christian commitment, Dean Munro developed numerous courses that were uniquely her own. Among them were "Literature by Types," "Ethical Problems in Literature," "The Sin Problem in Literature," and "The Bible as Literature."

Here, from her own classroom manuscript, we present the initial lecture from her course "The Bible as Literature."

The Bible as Literature

The Book of Books:
The Finger of God Writing a Book for Man

"In the presence of the Light of the world all other lights are dim, and it is impossible to consider the Bible merely as a literary work" (W. L. Phelps, *Human Nature in the Gospel*). But it is literature—literature unapproachable in form and content.

"The fact that works of perfect art are the media of the divine revelation furnishes a better proof of the inspiration of the Bible than the strongest dogmatic arguments or the most exact historical criticism could possibly supply" (Arthur J. Culler, *Creative Religious Literature*).

It has often been said that men cannot be well educated without the Bible. Nor can men be well read or cultured without the Bible. Books could be filled—some have been filled—with tributes to the literary excellence and power of the Bible, aside from its saving virtue.

"A Divine Library," said Jerome. "An infinite collection of the most varied and most venerable literature," said Edmund Burke. "Sunrise and sunset, birth and death, promise and fulfillment, the whole drama of humanity, are all in this book," said Heinrich Heine. "Wholly apart from its religious or from its ethical value, the Bible is the one Book that no intelligent person who wishes to come into contact with the world of thought and to share the ideas of the great minds of the Christian era can afford to be ignorant of. All modern literature and all art are permeated with it," said Charles Dudley Warner. All English literature is full of the Bible—Spenser, Shakespeare, Milton, Tennyson—Ruskin quotes the Bible 5,000 times in his writings. "It is almost impossible to exaggerate the influence of the English Bible upon our language."

Our purpose here it not to praise the Book but to read it together, to try to find out just what we mean when we eulogize the Bible as great literature. We shall try to define in simple terms the elements of literary power, and see how the Book we love proves itself. We shall find ourselves again and again forced to shout like old Sandy Scott, the Bible teacher, "I'm proud o' my Faither! I'm proud o' my Faither!"

Why did not God make the grass and the trees and the sky all one dirty drag? Why the glory of sunrise and sunset and the melting colors of the rainbow? Because He is the God of beauty as well as of righteousness; because holiness *is* beauty; because He always gives the best. So He has clothed His revelation of moral and saving truth in beautiful form—

the most beautiful of which human mind can conceive. And as we honor Him by appreciating the beauty of His handiwork in nature, so we honor Him by learning to appreciate the beauty and richness of the form of the Holy Scriptures.

We are used to hearing it said that the Bible is the world's greatest work of literature. We accept the fact but do not profit by it. In fact, we scarcely realize what it means—partly because we are not too clear as to what literature is anyway; partly, and more generally, because we read the Bible in a form that effectually conceals its literary character. Prof. Richard C. Moulton compares the effect of the usual printed form upon our appreciation of the literature of the Bible to the effect upon the vision of looking through a microscope that is out of focus. It is possible to calculate mentally what the picture should look like, but difficult and ineffective. To take the hurdle of the printed form I suggest that you use for this study Moulton's *Modern Reader's Bible,* which follows in the main the wording of the King James Version but prints poetry as poetry, essays as essays, stories as stories, and so on. And for the hurdle of literature, suppose we agree on what literature is.

Literature, they tell us, in the true sense is writing that does four things: (1) makes one think about life, (2) stirs the emotions, (3) kindles the imagination, and furthermore, (4) has power to survive. For example, history says in a bare statement of fact (2 Chron. 36:20): "And he carried them away to Babylon; and they were servants to him and his sons until the reign of the kingdom of Persia." Literature says, in the elegy of Psalm 137, "Babylon and Jerusalem":

I

By the rivers of Babylon,
There we sat down, yea, we wept,
When we remembered Zion.

199

Upon the willows in the midst thereof
We hanged up our harps.

For there they that led us captive
  required of us sons,
And they that wasted us required of us mirth:
  "Sing us one of the songs of Zion."
How shall we sing the Lord's song
In a strange land?

II

If I forget thee, O Jerusalem,
Let my right hand forget her cunning;
Let my tongue cleave to the roof of my mouth,
If I remember thee not;
If I prefer not Jerusalem above my chief joy.

And literature, they tell us, can do all these things for us:
(1) re-create the past—the *feel* of the Hebrew captivity in
Babylon; (2) make nature live for us—the willow trees over-
hanging the river; (3) acquaint us with human nature—the
homesick exiles taunted by their unfeeling captors; (4) keep
before us the vision of the ideal—hearts turned toward the
sanctuary, men learning through suffering that "above their
chief joy" they need God and His Church. No wonder their
song has lived through the generations. These men of the
Captivity, these displaced Jews of 2,500 years ago, were men
like their brothers of today, and their story has come alive to
us.

Literature has the power to survive. The greatest of all
short stories, "The Lost Boy" of Luke 15, will live as long as
time shall last; for, aside from its deathless expression of the
love of God, it embodies for all time the waywardness of
youth and the yearning tenderness of the father heart.

Another formula to express the living power of literature
is this: "Truth plus beauty equals immortality." That is, beau-

tiful words alone do not make the writing that lasts; to last, it must make us think truly about life; it must interpret life in some way. "Living thoughts in words that glow" is a good definition—or can words and thoughts be separated if they are true? The thought must be there, and a thought that is worth something to mankind. Prof. H. W. Garrod of Oxford University says that "life shakes us and rocks us," but a good book "stabilizes and confirms." Here the literature of the Bible tops every other favorite one can mention. Rather, it probes the depths of our natures; it opens great vistas before us; it is full of power, power under control.

To illustrate. Secular literature is full of lovely lyrics expressing a sense of the transitoriness of life. One of the most highly praised is by Robert Herrick (17th century), "To Daffodils."

> *Fair daffodils, we weep to see*
> *   You haste away so soon;*
> *As yet the early-rising sun*
> *   Has not attained his noon.*
> *   Stay, stay,*
> *   until the hasting day*
> *   Has run*
> *   But to the evensong;*
> *And, having prayed together, we*
> *   Will go with you along.*
>
> *We have short time to stay, as you;*
> *   We have as short a spring,*
> *As quick a growth to meet decay,*
> *   As you, or anything.*
> *   We die*
> *   As your hours do, and dry*
> *   Away*

> *Like to the summer's rain,*
> *Or as the pearls of morning's dew,*
> *Ne'er to be found again.*

Lovely indeed, and in its lilting lightness suggesting the light tossing of the flower on its stem and its fragile hold on life.

But what of its meaning? Incomplete. Its symbol of the shortness of life is itself borrowed from the Bible:

> As for man, his days are as grass:
> As a flower of the field, so he flourisheth.
> For the wind passeth over it, and it is gone;
> And the place thereof shall know it no more.
> —Ps. 103:15-16

The movement and the tone of the psalm breathe the sadness that is the truth about short-lived man when he lets himself think. That is, the form itself stirs the right emotion. And the poem continues with the strong, sturdy lines that leave us with the whole truth, not a segment of it:

> But the mercy of the Lord is from everlasting
> To everlasting upon them that fear him,
> And his righteousness unto children's children;
> To such as keep his covenant,
> And to those that remember his precepts to do them.
> —Ps. 103:17-18

The finest of all poems on this theme is the noble ode, "The Eternal God Thy Dwelling Place," Psalm 90.

Lord, thou hast been our dwelling place
In all generations.

Before the mountains were brought forth,
Or ever thou hast formed the earth and the world,
Even from everlasting to everlasting, thou art God.

Thou turnest man to dust;
  And sayest, Return, ye children of men.
For a thousand years in thy sight
  Are but as yesterday when it passeth,
  And as a watch in the night.
Thou carriest them away as with a flood;
  They are as a sleep.
In the morning they are like grass which groweth up.
  In the morning it flourisheth, and groweth up;
  In the evening it is cut down, and withereth.

For we are consumed in thine anger,
And in thy wrath are we troubled.

Thou hast set our iniquities before thee,
  Our secret sins in the light of thy countenance.
For all our days are passed away in thy wrath;
  We bring our years to an end as a tale that is told.
The days of our years are threescore years and ten,
  Or even by reason of strength fourscore years;
Yet is their pride but labour and sorrow;
  For it is soon gone, and we fly away.
Who knoweth the power of thine anger,
  And thy wrath according to the fear that is due unto thee?
  So teach us to number our days,
  That we may get us an heart of wisdom.

The steadying whole truth about the transitoriness of human life is seen only against the background of an eternal God. This poem makes us realize Him.

Set over against this the restrained, dignified, reverent, truly poetical because simple, beautiful, and true prose poem, the first chapter of Genesis. Hear the refrain of God's fiat, God's act, God's approval, God's rest; and your heart rests too.

In the beginning God created the heaven and
the earth. And the earth was waste and void; and

203

darkness was upon the face of the deep: and the spirit of God moved upon the face of the waters.

And God said, Let there be light: and there was light. And God saw that it was good: and God divided the light from the darkness. And God called the light Day, and the darkness he called Night. And there was evening and there was morning, one day.

And God said, Let there be a firmament in the midst of the waters, and let it divide the waters from the waters. And God made the firmament . . . and it was so. And God called the firmament Heaven. And there was evening and morning, a second day.

And God said, . . . Let the dry land appear: and it was so. And God called the dry land Earth . . . ; and God saw that it was good. And God said, Let the earth bring forth . . . and it was so. . . . And God saw that it was good. And there was evening and morning, a third day.

[And so on.] God said, Let there be lights . . . And there was evening and morning, a fourth day.

And God said, Let the waters bring forth abundantly, and let fowl fly above the earth in the firmament of heaven. . . . And there was evening and morning, a fifth day.

And God said, Let the earth bring forth the living creature after its kind . . . And God said, Let us make man in our image, after our likeness: and let them have dominion . . . And God blessed them . . . And God saw everything that he had made, and behold, it was very good. And there was evening and there was morning, the sixth day.

And the heaven and the earth were finished, and all the host of them. And on the seventh day God finished his work which he had made; and he rested on the seventh day from all his work which he had made. And God blessed the seventh day and hallowed it.

It does not clutter our minds with details, but it gives us God and harmony and eternal authority, and satisfaction of mind and heart—the rest of faith. It stabilizes by its revelation of God.

One last comparison for now, we shall find in two versions similiar story. The critics are fond of dubbing the Genesis stories "Hebrew myths" and so putting them on the same plane with the fantastic stories of the primitive Greeks and Babylonians. Some of the most beautiful and aesthetically pleasing bits of secular literature, with much of human appeal, are to be found in the Greek myths. But the fact of a God who is related to man in dependable moral responsibility—this same God-consciousness that we have seen in the lyric and in the didactic poetry—gives the Bible stories a fineness of texture and a depth of power and a spiritual dignity that the Greek myths lack. The myths are human notions; they cannot speak with assurance.

The stories I refer to are the two that deal with human sacrifice, the Greek myth of Agamemnon and Iphigenia and the Bible narrative of Abraham and Isaac. The Greek story is familiar. The ships of the Greek host ready to sail for Troy cannot get a favorable wind. It is learned that the leader Agamemnon has offended the goddess Artemis and can make atonement only by sacrificing his own daughter Iphigenia. He plunges the knife into her breast; fair weather follows and the ships set sail. Here we have thought about life—deep thought on a world that seems to run at cross-purposes; duties conflicting—to fulfill one's duty to God and country one must destroy one's own family; blind alleys and dead ends with no explanation; man apparently free to will but actually bound by an inscrutable fate. We are stirred to admire the great soul of man that dares face the unknown with head unbowed and look bravely into the darkness. But we are not satisfied. Freedom has no meaning unless the universe is moral and governed by intelligible moral principles. Man is degraded unless God is infinite in holiness.

So we turn with relief to the Bible story. Here we find the same command to sacrifice one's dearest at the will of God—but more cruel, even, for here the loss is an utter stripping; it involves the heir of promise. Here is the same obedience to the will of heaven—with a difference: the personal relationship and personal confidence of the man Abraham in a God whom he knows and trusts, who can be trusted to deliver and to provide. "God will provide himself a lamb" (Gen. 22:8). We catch the same note of triumph that sounds in the tortured Job's, "Though he slay me, yet will I trust in him" (Job 13:15); in the declaration of the three youths facing the fiery furnace, "Our God . . . is able to deliver . . . But if not, we will not [bow down]" (Dan. 3:17-18); in the apostle's ringing assurance, "Nay, in all these things we are more than conquerors through him that loved us" (Rom. 8:37). This is "to see life steadily and see it whole"—Matthew Arnold's famous tribute to Sophocles belongs of right only to the Christian who sees clear through to the end and out beyond, and sees only good because God is good. In the Christian philosophy there is no tragedy; there are no blind alleys, no dead ends. The story of Abraham and Isaac rings true to the deepest chords of human experience. It stabilizes heart and mind.

In the first chapter of his fine book *The English Bible as Literature,* Prof. C. A. Dinsmore quotes John Morley: "Literature consists of all the books—and they are not so many—where moral truth and human passion are touched with a certain largeness, sanity, and attraction of form." He places in the first rank three: Homer's *Iliad,* Dante's *Divine Comedy,* and Shakespeare's dramas, then shows the superiority of the Bible to each. The Bible surpasses Homer in scope and range as

206

the ocean surpasses a river. It surpasses Dante in universality. It surpasses Shakespeare in spiritual vision. As for variety and reality of character and dramatic power, when we include Christ and Calvary, secular literature has nothing to match it.

And its strongest claim to greatness is the background, or atmosphere, of the Eternal as an invisible presence, constantly at work, constantly realized, finally taking human form in the moment of crisis.

If the tests of great literature are the scope and quality of the humanized truth presented, the variety of emotions vividly and truthfully delineated in a manner at once generous, sane, and attractive, then the Scriptures certainly stand with the world classics. But if we add to these its effect on its readers, its power to liberate them from the drudgery of the commonplace, to add new territories to the domain of their consciousness, to move so powerfully on all their feelings as permanently to change their character, and to do this not to a few elect minds, but to all classes and conditions of men everywhere and in every age, then I think that we may claim for the English Bible a place not inferior to that occupied by the very greatest books of the Western World.

It seems we can be even more positive and assert that the Bible stands supreme.

We have sampled here and there; but the Bible—though we often read it so—is not a collection of fragments. It is a marvelous whole. To see it as literature we must see it not only as books, but as a Book. We must feel something of its majestic sweep.

"The English Bible is the production of a multitude of minds stretching in succession over nearly 3,000 years, representing many temperaments and many points of view. Like John at Patmos, we hear the voice of many waters, yet unified as the clear note of a trumpet. It is the Holy Ghost speaking in divers portions and in divers manners through many men, in many centuries, in many countries."

The Bible has the unity of the divine thought. "The sacred canon," to quote Dr. R. G. Moulton, "is not a mere Reading List, recommending the 66 Best Books of the Churches. These 66 books . . . are, when properly arranged, felt to draw together with a connectedness like the unity of a dramatic plot." And this unity is one that transcends all classification. To Professor Moulton the Old Testament is universal history, stretching from the beginning of the world to the first century of our era, offering a clear philosophy of world history. A chosen nation is prepared to be the "medium of the revelation of God to the other nations of the world"; only through captivity does it become a church conscious of its mission. All this is told in story, song, poetry, prophecy. Wisdom literature makes "a central pause in the movement" between the two Testaments. Then in the New Testament the coming of Christ and the kingdom of God at hand, an accelerated movement, a growing conception of the mission of His disciples. The narrative closes with Rome, "symbol of world unity"; the epilogue, the Apocalypse, "presents all history—past, present, and future—in one final conception: the kingdom of the world becoming the kingdom of our Lord and of His Christ."

Here is a growing, living organism, perfect in all its parts: the orations of Deuteronomy as fine as those of Cicero and fuller of human feeling; the idyll of Ruth more sincere and true than Theocritus; and so on.

The Finger of God Writing a Book for Men

As we begin our progress through this Book we find that what we have labeled "Bible history" is not formal history at all, but a framework in which are set numerous stories crammed full of human nature. One of the chief values claimed for literature is that it acquaints us with human nature. After all, people are more interested in people (in other personalities) than in anything else. And personality is the moving force of all the world. Reading the Bible, we find ourselves in a world alive with representative human beings, men and women just like ourselves and our neighbors and many others whom we have not yet seen but whom we may meet any day. And through their varied experiences we learn to know life. Here is the value of what we may call "vicarious experience" in literature: another lives for us a life for which we should not have time nor desire, and we reap the fruit in practical wisdom. That is, if the characters and the experiences are sufficiently typical, the Bible characters are superlatively so.

Suppose we stroll through some of the streets. How real these people are to us. Here is "Father Abraham," spiritual pioneer, who stakes all on heavenly values, who learns how to walk with God in unknown paths, how to conquer by faith and meekness. Here is Lot, who lives for this world and is betrayed by it, the "good businessman," the grasping opportunist whose "good bargain" proves a very poor one because he calculates for the short run.

Here is Esau, who "thinks more of his stomach than of his soul." "Odd, with Esau's example," says Frank S. Mead, "that men still prefer a ball game to an hour of prayer!" But they do.

And Jacob, the Bible "Jew": longheaded; shrewd, yet much enduring and fundamentally religious—the unlovely disposition that must have God's help to be decent. He has been called "Scripture's Dr. Jekyll and Mr. Hyde"—but God won out (Frank S. Mead).

Joseph the magnanimous, proving that simple goodness wins and forgiveness conquers.

Moses the executive, the brilliant-minded, the patriotic, the intensely human, whose achievement shows how largely God will use a prepared instrument.

Aaron, "eloquent but unstable," strong when he had a strong man to lean on, "a study in chaos."

Wholehearted Joshua, "an officer and a gentleman," who, "like Cromwell, carried the law in one hand and the sword in the other"—who in his youth followed the faith of his father Moses and in his maturity followed "the Man with the drawn sword," and so in his old age challenged a nation to commit itself to God.

Some of these figures are drawn full length; many others are flashed before us in a phrase or a characteristic gesture: Caleb, the brave warrior, who "wholly followed the Lord," and who in old age demanded, "Give me this mountain" to conquer (Josh. 14:8-9, 12); Achan, the cowardly sinner, who stole and must hide his booty. He got for his sin only the pile of stones that covered his dead body—and ruined his family to boot.

Balaam the compromiser, who "had the gift but lacked the grace of a great prophet."

Gideon, "a boy who tore down altars"—doing wonders when he dared to step out on the word of God, but cautious and testing every plank to see if it would hold.

Samson, the Bible Hercules or "champion athlete" (W. L. Phelps) and the Bible practical joker. Strong in brawn, weak in brain, good-natured, living by instinct. But he learned. And God used him.

Eli, the old man, loving the ark and letting his children go to the dogs.

Samuel the puritan, loyal to God and duty in an age of laxness, but more—reformer, recalling his nation to God and faith. "Israel's Man of the Hour . . . was being summoned" when God called "Samuel, Samuel." "King-maker, rebuilder, government centralizer, national unifier, dispeller of decadence—Samuel! There walked a man" (F. S. Mead).

Saul the tragic—fine, handsome, modest young country fellow with the magnetic personality and the kingly bearing. But the throne is too much for him. He grows "drunk with power" and counts God out. Jealous of a rival, he fights insanely to keep his footing. But God has forsaken him; and the mighty falls.

The many-sided David: warrior, administrator, poet, hero—great saint and great sinner—great lover of God, and great in the bigness of his humanity—"God so loved him that he built him a house, gave him a Messiah for a son" (F. S. Mead).

And so they pass in review: Jonathan the loyal son and the perfect friend; Nathan the fearless, who dared tell a king the unpalatable truth; Absalom, the fascinating, handsome schemer who stole men's hearts. Solomon "glitters with the bigness—and it hides him." He had unmatched opportunity and threw it away—and in his old age, disillusioned, he wrote Ecclesiastes. "'All is vanity' is his Great Amen." Jeroboam, the politically ambitious—"He helped a nation to lose its soul. He set no value on God's favor; God set not value on him." Ahab, the moral coward; Elijah, "stouthearted, thunder-voiced," "lone wolf of the Lord"—"a man of like passions as we," yet strong in the consciousness of God. "The Lord God before whom I stand," was his slogan; fire was his symbol. Elisha, follower but not copier of his master Elijah; milder, more cultured, but as undeviating in his loyalty to truth and wearing the same mantle of spiritual power.

Nehemiah the builder, cool brain and hot heart; Daniel the daring—and steadfast. But we cannot begin to complete the roll call of the Old Testament—and there stretch John the Baptist and John the Beloved and Peter and Paul and Stephen and . . .

211

Professor Phelps in his book *Reading the Bible* tells of the chaplain in World War I who was relating to the men on a transport the story of Paul's shipwreck and his two weeks in a typhoon. "Who was that guy?" asked one. "A man named Paul." Going back to the cabin he roused his bunkie: "Chaplain was telling us a story about a fellow named Paul, and he was some man." The Bible characters are our contemporaries!

As for the women of the Bible—Bruce Barton before writing his best-seller, *The Book Nobody Knows,* took a poll of 10,000 preachers to select 10 famous women of the Bible. Seventy-four different names were suggested. Those chosen were Eve, Ruth, Hannah, the woman called "great," Esther, Mary the mother of Jesus, Mary Magdalene, the Bethany sisters, the woman of Samaria, the widow who gave the two mites. So much for the "famous." But how real they all are—real and broadly typical.

Here is Miriam, the clever, affectionate big sister, glorying in her brother's triumphs, but feeling entitled by relationship and ownership to grumble and criticize. Here is Rahab the innkeeper, the "scarlet woman" with the generous heart, who believes and saves the men of God. She becomes the mother of Boaz and ancestress of Jesus.

Here is Deborah, the "mother in Israel" and the militant crusader against national evil—wise and courageous and tireless, daring where men cowered—a Hebrew Frances Willard or Joan of Arc. And Jael, the bold assassin of the enemy of her cause, who brought him butter, then drove a spike through his temples, Charlotte Corday of her time.

Delilah, the heartless "secret agent," employing her charms to entrap the unwary general on the enemy side; Naomi, the warmhearted, longheaded schemer for good—her hurt heart healed by a baby's touch, her grandson's. Orpah, the very natural girl, full of life, not ready to bury herself alive; and Ruth, the self-forgetful, living for love and duty and God.

212

Here is Hannah, the praying mother who wants her boy to be a missionary; Rizpah, the bereaved mother, fiercer than a lioness robbed.

David's three wives: Michal, "the eternal feminine," perverse, willful, proud of her husband so long as he puts her first, but jealous of God himself; Abigail, the capable and considerate, provider and manager; Bathsheba, of easy morals and easy winning.

Jezebel, the Lady Macbeth of the Bible, daring where her husband was weak, but stronger and wickeder—a religious fanatic, queen to her fingertips; and Athaliah her daughter, made of the same stuff, bold and bad, determined to rule, less vain and more ruthless—all steel. An unscrupulous woman, worse than an unscrupulous man.

Other queens—Vashti, the modest and independent; Esther, the courageous, self-sacrificing, and loyal. And the hospitable Shunamite woman who kept the prophet's chamber, the woman called "great"—wealthy and using her wealth to entertain God's servants.

And so on to the New Testament with its Marys and its Joanna, its Dorcas and Lydia, its Lois and Eunice—and its Herodias and Salome.

But the best way to study botany is to gather flowers; the best way to study human nature in the Bible is to read for oneself. Frank S. Mead's fascinating *Who's Who in the Bible* contains 250 thumbnail sketches of different individuals. William Lyon Phelps's *Human Nature in the Bible* and *Human Nature in the Gospel* are alive with real people. And all these only in the Bible narrative. The poetry and drama and philosophy of the Book are likewise rammed and crammed with life. No wonder; for the Book was written by the Creator who made no two men alike and who knows the men He has made. It was written about man and for man, and it shows man himself as does no other book.

213

12

The Years
Still Teach

"The Best of Bertha Munro" has been recorded through her writing in the pages of this book. Or has it?

In terms of mature Christian thought, informed by a lifetime of study of the Bible and literature, and presented in written form, her finest insights again have inspired, blessed, and instructed us. But a full understanding of the "best" of such a person can be known only as her conduct in the "crucible of life" proves consistent with the precepts of her writings.

Thus finally we seek to catch a glimpse of Bertha Munro's later years; years of retirement and declining health; years of continuing determination to know God's purpose for her *now* and to fulfill it. Her Lord, she was convinced, had given her a task, and she was determined to do His will.

Her task? To write yet another book, a companion to her autobiography *The Years Teach,* to be titled "The Years Still Teach." And of even greater importance, to "spread joy," sharing with others the great joy Christ had placed within her heart. Hear her words:

> I used to pray, "Dear Lord, make any use You can of me, but don't throw me on the scrap heap." Now He has reminded me, "God will not waste a consecrated life." Listening, I knew His voice: "You will live just as long as I have a use for you"; and I am at rest.

> So, it looks as if I shall never be "retired," free to be shut in, to read, to do doublecrostics and wander endlessly through my prized collection of great art. For yesterday I had my choice: "I'm over 90 now and almost through," or "I may live to be 100." The decision is God's; the mental attitude is mine.

> Which reminds me, I'd better get at that assignment He gave me a few years ago and I haven't found time to do much with: "The Years Still Teach."

217

Here I am beginning to do a job I have faced for months. The fact is that I have been commissioned to do something with an outline I had started for a work I should probably never write.

I had better stop here. I have just now opened the "turtle box" where I have outlines of the past five years to find that they all say the same thing in different words. Always about His love for me and my love for Him and always the same outline. *Her joy!*

It came to me the other day by way of a lift of spirit to express and make definite my daily commitment and commission for these later days. Prayer, yes—and try to comfort and encourage. Now it is "sharing joy," which means *always having* joy to share—maintaining joy in my own heart. "His joy" and "count it all joy," "the joy of the Lord is your strength"—there is my supply available and it must be singing: "Lord, *sing* that joy through me to saddened lives."

Spreading joy and writing yet another book—twin tasks, God-given, for a 90-year-old! The "turtle box" of which she speaks had been given her full of candy by an admiring former student who remembered her mentor's famed sweet tooth. The box, soon emptied, became a repository for notes for her new book. In typical Munro fashion, the notes were sketchy, later to be fleshed out and made complete.

"The Years Still Teach" was to revolve around Miss Munro's philosophy of life, which she called "The Munro Doctrine." Its words were found in her own script on a scrap of paper beside her chair during the last years of her life:

> Truth Cannot Contradict Truth
> God Will Not Waste a Consecrated Life
> Persons Are More than Things

Not Somehow, but Triumphantly
The Listening Heart

There is a sense in which "The Munro Doctrine" stands alone and needs no explanatory words, but it appears that Bertha Munro had planned to expand on each thought in the chapters of her proposed book. Here are some samples of her thinking:

On Truth

> To be truly an integrated Christian, loving God with all the mind is not an easy achievement, but we must never doubt that in Christ we have the best, that is, the source of all the best. And we have the Holy Spirit to make Him real in our lives. We have met Him in deliverance from the guilt and power of sin; we do well to explore and share what we have found of His relevance as *truth for today.*

On God's Use of Consecrated Lives

> "God will not waste a consecrated life"—how often I have repeated this to a young person uncertain of God's will for his choice of a life's vocation. I have trusted it for myself and depended on it and have found that with changing circumstances God gives a new assignment. Throughout my life I have lived joyfully through ups and downs, through "circumstance," knowing that I would want to live only as long as God had some use for me. But suppose the time would come when He had to "throw me on the scrap heap."

> I have known of good Christians who in their later years become grouchy and hard to live with. Not that! Yet I hope the Lord could still use something that I could do. Prayer perhaps. But suppose all my faculties gave out; I was "just a vegetable"—I would so hope not that!

And just at that time I came across a book by Edna Hardy, *Turn Over Any Stone.* Live in the will of God, and every tragedy will have two sides; turn it over and you find Jesus there. The book contains the beautiful story of a Christian woman's determined search and finding faith's answer. Her personal tragedy was the birth of a granddaughter with a totally useless brain—brought into the world to live, with nothing to live with.

Reading the book was a long, slow journey, but for me the last pages spoke the words *I* needed. She recalled an educated Christian gentleman, her father's friend, who in his last days suffered mental loss. Words jumbled. Meaningless. Friends commiserated. Pitied. God saw that those tangled words formed a liturgy of praise. He said, "It is good." People said, "How painful. What tragedy." God said, "It is good."

But finally everything was gone but an empty frame; a vast emptiness. His friends grieved. God saw a vast "emptiness of givenness," and He said, "It is good."

This was my answer. I have no more questions about the future, for all I know is that I want to live only as God has some use for me—in whatever form.

Persons Are More than Things

Searching the turtle box, we find that Miss Munro apparently had not yet written concerning this part of the Munro Doctrine; but a tribute to Bertha Munro delivered by Dr. Samuel Young at Founders' Day at Eastern Nazarene College in 1968, makes the concept plain.

She never taught a class—she taught individuals. Even when classes became large, she seemed to

220

know them one by one. She had the happy faculty of adding a name to each one that described him for what he was or did. It may have sounded like a nickname to some, but it wasn't. It was descriptive and appallingly accurate. In evaluating her own service, she never pandered to an *A* student to the neglect of the *C* student.

For many years she gave thumbnail sketches of the seniors at the Junior-Senior Banquet, and many individuals received a deserving and revealing boost or a gentle stab with good humor . . . in truth, her students became her children, and their children, in turn, became her grandchildren too. And when they left these halls, she followed them with personal notes, especially during holiday seasons, even to faraway places, reassuring them especially in times of crisis that she still loved, cared, prayed, and understood.

Not Somehow, but Triumphantly

Bertha Munro early cultivated the habit of an early morning tryst with God—a time of prayerful meditation when God gave her His song for the day ahead. She speaks of the morning hours:

Every morning early I listen for His first word to me: first the song that I wake up with, then thought, scripture, direction for the day.

"Thou wilt keep him in perfect peace, whose mind is stayed on thee" (Isa. 26:3). That peace (beyond human understanding) James described as ["peace-loving" wisdom]: "pure, . . . submissive, . . . good, . . . sincere" (3:17, NIV). The "stayed mind" is the set of the will, the attitude of steadfast trust. The promise of the blessing sought is not an emotion but a holy heart; not a temporary feeling but a perma-

221

nent quality of spirit. It is, if we will have it, the deep peace of eternity. I listened one day, and for a moment I thought I breathed its atmosphere. This peace will "keep our hearts and minds" (cf. Phil. 4:7).

I am drawn to God's first word of revelation in His approach to man—even before His creation. "Let there be light" (Gen. 1:3). Breaking the darkness, the Eternal Son purposing with the Father—and the God-man Jesus kneeling in Gethsemane, the pattern of our redemption, a divine-human undertaking that would last into eternity to bridge the gap between justice and mercy. The immensity of the endless sweep in time and space are the issues, but also the breathtaking power of the human will, Spirit-filled: "I sink by dying love compelled and own Thee conqueror."

My will shall choose as Jesus the Man chose. The significance of a single choice. I must remember when I am facing a crucial choice, that choice of God's will—"Thy will be done" (cf. Luke 22:42)—is not to be made as to a trial in resignation; but in confidence and in thanksgiving to the Giver and gratitude for the gift of His assured blessing.

The Listening Heart

"I will run the way of thy commandments, when thou shalt enlarge my heart" (Ps. 119:32).

"I will instruct thee and teach thee in the way which thou shalt go: I will guide thee with mine eye" (Ps. 32:8).

David's prayer began to be answered for me the day I saw that my vital Christian life was more than the *state*—genuine as it was—of a sanctified heart expressing itself in sanctified living. It was a personal *relationship* with God in Jesus to be maintained and developed by a constant communication, ever fresh, increasingly intimate. This communication is a matter of the heart that loves and is eager to know "the will of God" in order to give Jesus a gift that will satisfy His desires.

God is always sending out messages: "The wind of the Spirit is blowing." The air is electric with them, only waiting for the right "radio" to pick them up or the right receiver to tune in. He will direct the willing listener. There are no chance contingencies or coincidences.

I found this true at the time of the General Assembly in Dallas in 1976 [Dean Munro had been praying for unity in the church]. One day as I was praying for the imminent assembly in Dallas, that request was stopped by the very real question, "What's the use of one person praying for a crowd like that?" I was in earnest and my faith couldn't stretch. The answer came as I listened: "You can pray for *individuals* to be filled with the Spirit in a fresh new way." And, at the vast opening Communion Service I heard (listening) Dr. Lawlor, general superintendent in charge, open the service with the impassionate plea to pause in prayer; for individuals to remember that Communion is not for a mass —a group, an organization—it is for *individuals*.

My heart sang, and throughout the days following I had opportunity to see that the organization of our church has proved essential, especially for "foreign" overseas new countries that are losing their missionaries but can carry on by themselves; they have been prepared for self-government. The machinery has been oiled by the

Spirit living in individuals. And later actions—grace for an international church with the adopted watchword "Life in the Spirit" speak to me of the real unity that is God's concern. Those words of Dr. Lawlor in the opening convention may sound like coincidence; many so-called coincidences (if we could see) all would have another name: "God at work."

Latter Days

As age took its toll, Bertha Munro's doctor advised that she needed the professional care that only a nursing home could give. Because of her rugged Scottish individualism, coupled with years of life in old New England, the transition was difficult. In typical fashion she relied on the Lord and came ultimately to see her confinement under loving care as another of His gifts to her. Literally hundreds of her former students, colleagues, and friends came regularly to see her, leaving with the feeling that they who had come to be a blessing were the ones who went away blessed. Because of infirmity, she seldom now could attend services in the Wollaston Church of the Nazarene where she had worshiped for so many years. One Sunday evening, feeling stronger, she insisted on going to church where her nephew was preaching in revival services. As she sat in her wheelchair, someone asked what song she would like the congregation to sing. Without hesitation, she replied, "Joy to the world! the Lord is come." And so, together we sang a Christmas carol in mid-May!

When in January 1983 it became evident that the time of her crossing "to a more excellent glory" was near, friends and family stood by. One day when a time of agitation came upon her, the little group by her bedside began to sing. Immediately she calmed, brightened, and her lips began to form the words:

> *Amazing grace! how sweet the sound!*
> *That saved a wretch like me!*
> *I once was lost, but now am found;*
> *Was blind, but now I see.*

And, from that time until that holy moment when, as her pastor put it, "in a roomful of angels" she went to be with her Lord, her loved ones literally sang her into heaven. They sang "Amazing Grace" over and over again, "I Know I Love Thee Better, Lord," "When I Survey," "Yes, I Know," "In the Garden," "Blessed Assurance," and "The Comforter Has Come." She especially enjoyed her favorite third verse:

> *Lo, the great King of Kings, with healing in His wings,*
> *To every captive soul a full deliverance brings;*
> *And through the vacant cells the song of triumph rings:*
> *The Comforter has come!*

In the funeral home and at the church, her former students and colleagues maintained a 24-hour honor guard by her side. She had planned the service herself, stating that she desired that the spirit of the service be "joyful—no meaning to sorrow here!" It was to be filled with song. By her instruction, the organist played "The Comforter Has Come," "Day by Day," "Ho! Every One That Is Thirsty," "I Know I Love Thee Better, Lord," and "Joy to the World." Her niece played "Amazing Grace" as a violin solo. The congregation joined in "How Firm a Foundation" and "And Can It Be?" The A Cappella Choir from her own Eastern Nazarene College sang "All the Way My Savior Leads Me," "Be Still, My Soul," "When I Survey," and "He Hideth My Soul." Soloists—former students—sang "The Crystal Fountain" and "Until Then." And her nephew, Dr. Stephen W. Nease, president of Eastern

Nazarene College, preached a gospel message based on John 17:13, "His Joy Fulfilled!"

At the graveside the next day, her pastor, Rev. Russell Metcalfe, led in reading the 23rd psalm, ending the graveside service with the Lord's Prayer and in singing, one final time, "Amazing Grace."

Her pastor's committal prayer still speaks to the hearts of those who said farewell that day:

It isn't that we don't have more words; it is just that we know we can never say it all . . . and it is time to say, "Good-bye!" *But not forever!*

We have come as far as we humanly can in love and respect for the house in which Bertha Munro lived, and now we commit her frail, worn-out body to the grave. The ritual says, "Earth to earth, ashes to ashes . . ."

But we know that we shall see her again, in glory unimaginable—in the bright light of heaven we shall meet!

And until that day, I pray that something of the spirit of Bertha Munro will live in the memory of each of us; that we will love God's kingdom a little better, and love each other a little more, and love God with a total abandon . . . and that we shall pick up her task of spreading Christ's *joy!*

A Final Testimony

In 1977, Dr. J. Kenneth Grider of Nazarene Theological Seminary recorded an interview with Bertha Munro that is titled "Our Church: Memories and Forecasts of a 90-Year-

Old." After responding faithfully to the perceptive questions of the interviewer, Bertha Munro adds what she calls an "Addendum." In reality, it is her personal testimony and perhaps best summarizes *The Best of Bertha Munro.*

I still believe that a simple, direct message on the second crisis in the old, familiar language, *under the anointing of the Holy Spirit,* will produce genuine revival results. But success will not be due to the specific terms used; rather, to the complete dependence on the opened heavens—kept open by prayer and faith. For the crisis is central. Jesus gave himself for His Church that He might sanctify it. And I still hear Dr. J. B. Chapman's statement that only if at least 51 percent of the members of the Church of the Nazarene possess this sanctifying experience, is it a holiness church.

"State" or "relationship"? Gift or the Giver himself? Thanks given or praises sung? *Both.* And always must be. God has always spoken to people in "accommodated terms"—words they could understand. The Spirit knows how to fit message to hearers, "perfect love" or "entire sanctification."

When it comes to my own "personal satisfactions"—at the deep core of the joy of His assured presence is the certain assurance given me years ago, and still alive as I "trust and obey," that my heart is free from that old carnal nature—in me a special brand of self-centeredness. And in the hour of temptation I still need that assurance.

I recall too the day of my overwhelming, unexpected joy in the realization that my most intense delight was to be in the center of God's will and to know that I knew that to be my joy. Infinite regress of assurance! And variety of expression!

Resource Notes

Sources of the material used in chapters 1 through 9 are cited below. When material in chapters 10 through 12 is attributed to Miss Munro, it comes from varied writings by her, unpublished manuscripts, and conversations.

Chapter 1

Truth for Today. Kansas City: Beacon Hill Press, 1947.

Chapter 2

Not Somehow, but Triumphantly: Talks to Young People. Kansas City: Beacon Hill Press, 1950.

Chapter 3

The Pilgrim's Road Map: Studies in "Pilgrim's Progress." Kansas City: Beacon Hill Press, 1950.

Chapter 4

Strength for Today. Kansas City: Beacon Hill Press, 1954.

Chapter 5

The Years Teach: Remembrances to Bless. Kansas City: Beacon Hill Press of Kansas City, 1970.

"Their Gift to Me," *The Christian Scholar,* February 1983.

"Success," *One in the Bond of Love.* Kansas City: Beacon Hill Press of Kansas City, 1984.

Chapter 6

Shining Pathway. Kansas City: Beacon Hill Press of Kansas City, 1974.

Chapter 7

One in the Bond of Love.

Chapter 8

"Gifts," "Thanks Be unto God for His Unspeakable Gift," "Epiphany," "As He Said," from *The Years Teach.*

"Great Joy," from *One in the Bond of Love.*

Chapter 9

"The Risen Christ Recognized," *Come Ye Apart* (April, May, June, 1963).

"Good News of Peace," *Come Ye Apart* (October, November, December, 1963).

"Changed," *Herald of Holiness,* March 23, 1960.

"The Ancient Beautiful Things," *Herald of Holiness,* February 17, 1971.

"The Bible," *Lift Up Thine Eyes: 111 Meditations Selected from "Come Ye Apart."* Kansas City: Beacon Hill Press of Kansas City, 1969.

"Preaching in the Early Days of the Holiness Movement," *The Nazarene Preacher,* April 1968.

"Channels, Not Cisterns," *Sunrise Devotions: By and for Retirees.* Kansas City: Beacon Hill Press of Kansas City, 1978.